A WHOLE NEW BALL GAME

A WHOLE NEW BALL GAME

PHIL DE GLANVILLE
WITH LEONARD STALL

MAINSTREAM
PUBLISHING

EDINBURGH AND LONDON

First published in Great Britain in 1997 by
MAINSTREAM PUBLISHING COMPANY (EDINBURGH) LTD
7 Albany Street
Edinburgh EH1 3UG

ISBN 1 85158 976 7

A catalogue record for this book is available from the British Library
Printed and bound in Great Britain by Butler & Tanner Ltd, Frome

To Yolanda and my family, with love

CONTENTS

ACKNOWLEDGEMENTS

Thanks to Julia Goatcher for all her hard work transcribing hours and hours of taped conversation; Maria Bowers and Roger Marshall at Medialab for their researching, reading and re-reading; Mick Cleary, now of the *Daily Telegraph*; Cellnet; Fiona Foster at Karen Earl Ltd; Ashley Woolfe of the James Grant Group; Ken Johnstone at Bath RFC; Peter Hall; all of the other hard-working national newspaper rugby correspondents not mentioned here. Time fades the memory. If we have any of the dates, names, times and places a little wrong, our apologies.

Special thanks to my family, who put up with me tapping at the laptop at all times of day and night. Geneviève and Sebastian, I love you!

LEONARD STALL
MAY 1997

De Glanville in Control

By Mick Cleary,
rugby correspondent of the *Daily Telegraph*

'Phil de Glanville has the smooth, unassuming looks of a corporate executive. He is unthreatening, affable and completely stripped of ego. He is no Willie John McBride, Buck Shelford or Sean Fitzpatrick. He does not make you take a step back at first meeting, tremble as he gives you the first stare. He's a back, for goodness sake. Small wonder he was variously dubbed 'Hollywood' and 'Pretty' when he first pitched up at Bath from Oxford University. But Bath took him on. They know that actions, not superficial impressions, define character.'

You want a journalist to write a foreword? About a player? And not just any old player but the England captain to boot – the high-profile, celebrity-with-knobs-on, well-groomed, PR-desirable icon of the professional era, at a time in the game when all is change, traditions are jettisoned and a clear line is marked between them on one side and us lot on the other. The player and the journo, the star and the hack, and never the twain shall meet unless it's in the antiseptic, clinically controlled environment of the press conference, the theatre of the soundbite where pat answer meets predictable question and the dead bat is played to the tabloid rottweiler's verbal throat-ball.

It may come as a surprise to those on the outside to learn that we on the inside do actually talk to each other as human beings as well. And, whisper it gently, it has even been known for drink to be taken on occasions when our worlds collide outside the sporting arena. In fact, drink is sometimes taken when we're technically on the job, although the strictures of the professional age threaten to restrict the drinking habits of one of the parties concerned. It won't be us lot who forsake heritage, I can tell you.

No, it's a great relief to those who value the old ways of the world (or the important ones, at any rate) to see that the gulf between player and journalist which exists in soccer and is becoming increasingly marked in cricket has not yet appeared in rugby. There are occasional cracks, with tensions at times, but these are no more than natural occurrences in any relationship in any workplace. (Although I must admit that when Graham Dawe drew up a chair late one night at a post-match banquet at Toulouse with the express object of grilling the *Telegraph*'s John Reason as to precisely why he thought he was a bloody useless hooker, you did wonder whether you should dive in to protect your journalistic colleague. Curiosity, not to mention a shameful, deep-rooted liking for punch-ups, suppressed any inclination to intervene. Good old JR survived – and for that hundreds of players up and down the land have cursed Dawesy ever since.)

Performer and critic have always had an uneasy association, akin, as it was once famously said, to that of a lamppost viewing the approach of a dog. This is where Phil has coped brilliantly with his first year in office. He knew when he accepted Jack Rowell's invitation to be England captain that it might well be a bumpy ride. It was. And DG copped an awful lot of criticism *en route*, not least from those shuffling the deck to sort out the British Lions squad for South Africa. There were no end of aspic-dipped pens having their two pennyworth, too. Phil de Glanville lacked pace, cutting edge, creative touch (see, they've got me at it now), and given that Jeremy Guscott was playing the most sublime rugby of his life, wasn't worth his place in the side. DG took it all in his stride. Personally I would have cracked and smacked the living daylights out of someone at some point. But Phil saw the comments for what they were: perspectives on his game, the written embodiment of what was being said by someone somewhere on the terraces. He recognised that everyone has an opinion and that only rarely in sport will opinions converge unanimously to reach the same conclusion. That is the whole point of sport. It takes us away from the black and white of ordinary life into an emotional make-believe world where we can live out our fantasies through those talented enough to represent them on the field of play. As spectators we criticise because we care passionately.

Phil accepted too that newspapers have to line up more or less with public opinion. Papers can shape opinion, set agendas, influence judgements, even top-spin the truth but, by and large, if they get out of kilter too often then pretty soon they will find themselves as a newspaper without readers. Phil admitted that he wasn't in very good form, the irony being that 12 months earlier, when he felt he was in the best form of his life, it was de Glanville on the bench and Carling and Guscott on the field. Phil put up with it for years, denied a fair crack of the whip because a dimple-chinned bloke by the name of Carling was in the slot as captain. Captaincy in its own right was considered important all through the Carling reign. And it should still be considered so now.

I don't agree with those who think that the job has been devalued in modern times by the advent of special coaches, video analysis and choreographed play where the number of options to be stored away at any one time increasingly resembles American Football. What need is there for a captain when the key decisions have already been taken in the build-up to matches either by the coaches or by the pivotal players on the pitch itself? The answer is still every need. Every side needs a focus, a sense of character, to shape it, define it and give it inner strength and belief. It needs a calm head, too, when the pre-match playbook filled with all these fancy theories of how the game will evolve proves to be completely useless the moment the first whistle blows and those unthreatening chalk marks on the training blackboard become elusive, fast-moving, intimidating and very real human lumps of muscle. The captain is the man in the eye of the storm, the one to spot what is happening and alter course accordingly. The sceptics are right when they say the days of sleeves-rolled-up, retaliation-in-first, fight-'em-on-the-beaches days of captaincy are over. They are entirely wrong when they say there is no need for leaders like Phil de Glanville.

There is a maturity, stability and presence about Phil which will imbue any team. And look again at the neatly turned-out, bright-eyed, handsome, pleasant, well-mannered young chap in front of you. Look more closely at those eyes gleaming merrily. For when those eyes start to narrow, that is when you are in trouble. Or the opposition is. Phil de Glanville is a competitive beast: hard-edged, ruthless and with nerves as hard as diamond. He can be sharp and caustic if the occasion merits it, uncompromising and stone-hearted in tight corners. He fought the good fight for all it was worth in the protracted club versus union dispute, making sure that the issues were confronted and the best deal was hammered out for all concerned, not just the pampered few (such as himself) at the top end of the game.

Phil was embroiled in a very nasty bout of domestic bickering down at Bath where the family which prided itself on resilience and togetherness suddenly disintegrated. It was internecine war. People such as Brian Ashton and John Hall, guys Phil knew well as colleagues and as friends, fell out and went their separate ways. It was a time of acute crisis for Bath: in chaos off the field and shambling on it. The thumping cup defeat at home to Leicester was the lowest point in the club's modern history. It took real resolve not to fold under such pressure. I never saw Phil lose control for a second.

On the field he is one of the most fearless players I've come across. He's far from the biggest international centre in the world but he tackles as if he is. He is also the best chaser and harrier of a high ball in the game, a selfless, unglamorous role if ever there was one.

And he's a nice bloke too. It may not appear to count for much in these days of sport as a glorified balance sheet, with achievement and meaning measured purely in terms of profit and loss. But it does. Character and politeness and intelligence and affability and integrity and decency ought to matter. It ought to matter, too, that you can relate to these people, have enough respect for one another to disagree with each other and yet still be civilised and matey in company. With Phil there is never any question of a journalist betraying his trust. Off-the-record comments are kept strictly off-the-record. This does not mean that things are covered up or critical thoughts held back; just that private moments remain private.

So I can't tell you about the three members of the England touring party in South Africa in 1994 whom I had to bankroll at a Pretoria casino late one night as the roulette wheel insisted on spinning my way not theirs. It cost one of them his entire tour allowance (Barnesy had already spent his – oops). I can't reveal either the name of the player spotted stumbling out of the Rugby Writers' Dinner (or its aftermath) one year and trying to hitch-hike a lift from a milk float in central London at 5.30 a.m., anxious to get home for a few hours' kip before England training began at midday. No, I can't tell you his name because he, too, is a good bloke. And good blokes sometimes drink and fall over and have fun and no one gets hurt or inconvenienced. I hasten to add that I've never (or maybe that should be not often) come across Phil de Glanville in such a condition. But if I did I'd pick him up, dust him down, send him on his way and never breathe a word of it. Because he is a damn fine bloke and that's why I feel immensely honoured to have been asked to write these few words about him.

MICK CLEARY
MAY 1997

On the Inside

After such a momentous year or so, it's great to have the opportunity to put pen to paper. Top-class rugby has been in turmoil, and the very fabric of the senior game has altered on and off the field. Indeed it is 'a whole new ball game' – and I've seen the upheaval from the inside.

I became the England captain, and my emerging young side won the Triple Crown – and so very nearly a Grand Slam. But, after winning the double in my first season in charge at Bath, we had a frustrating 1996–97 campaign with nothing to show for our efforts. The trophy cabinet is empty, and we don't like it!

Jack Rowell deserves a mention in these pages, and he gets it, and so too do characters like Bath's John Hall and Brian Ashton, Cliff Brittle of the RFU and good old Fran Cotton. Jerry Guscott and a few of my teammates also come in for a little gentle stick. The pen certainly is mightier than the sword!

Rugby is a changing game, and the life of a rugby player has been transformed beyond all recognition during the last year. The rapid changeover to the professional rugby union code has brought new opportunities on a flood tide of cash, but it has multiplied, many times over, the strains on the generally backward administration of the sport. The RFU's running battle with English Professional Rugby Union Clubs Ltd, EPRUC, was the most public sign of the tensions. If only the RFU had reacted to the onset of professionalism by seeing it as an opportunity rather than as a threat we could have avoided all of the wrangling, and administrators and clubs could have moved on hand in hand to make the most of what the modern game has to offer. That was not to be, however, and the on-going — and at times bitter — arguments caused the sport much pain. But at club level too the cracks began to show, with the administration of the sport here falling way behind the changing game on the pitch: a new, open and perhaps more exciting game which has caught the imagination of the rugby public.

And, while some Courage League Division One and Two players have managed to accept, embrace and benefit from professionalism, moving forward into the new era along with some of their clubs, others have struggled to cope with the more stringent demands being placed upon them by the need for an increasingly full-time commitment to rugby.

Personally, I am still walking the thin line between a career and being a full-time professional sportsman. It's good for me as a person, because I still feel the need to have a life — a working life — outside of the game I love, but I certainly couldn't have done it without the help, support and understanding of my wife, Yolanda, and the extraordinary flexibility and generosity of Druid, the company that now employs me. I also have the determination and self-motivation to be able to juggle the complex demands of work and professional sport together with those of my personal life, at least for the moment.

A few of my teammates and friends in the game have found the transition much more demanding. When rugby union took its first faltering steps into the world of professionalism, some of the players who wanted to carry on 'as normal' began to find it increasingly difficult to balance the demands of work and rugby, and not surprisingly so; their jobs were just not flexible enough to cope with the sport's new training schedules. There were also problems in store for some of the players who gave up their careers and turned to full-time rugby, as a handful struggled to come to terms with the increased personal commitment and self-motivation required by the new professional game. At the beginning of the season there were still a few players who couldn't find the extra motivation needed to change their deeply ingrained approach to what had been an amateur game for as long as they could remember. Those players stood out like a sore thumb. They may have been professional in name but their approach to the new code was anything but professional, and they were clearly finding it impossible to reorganise their lives accordingly. That lack of planning and self-discipline was disappointing. In fact, I had frequently seen more evidence of their motivation and commitment when they were busy with their business careers. Back then, when we were playing for silver rather than silver and gold, these players were ready to turn up at the crack of dawn for a club training session. But once they had turned into professional sportsmen and resigned from the duties of their salaried day jobs, it left them with too much time on their hands – which drained away their self-discipline. Admittedly, as the season progressed most of these footballers gradually came to terms with the rigours of the professional code. However, there are still one or two lagging behind who have yet to sort themselves out.

The 1996–97 season was a tough one, particularly at Bath RFC, where we had more than our fair share of trouble and interruption. And while it was a difficult time off the field, on it our long dominance of the club game evaporated, almost overnight. It was inevitable, I suppose, with the advent of professionalism giving rival clubs the money and incentive to invest in bringing some of the world's best players to grace the UK game.

Our stranglehold of the domestic league and cup competitions is a fond memory for now, but we still came close to glory in the league, and in the Heineken European Clubs Cup. And we were only knocked out of the Pilkington Cup by an on-song Leicester side, in what was the low point of our club season. Bearing in mind the changes which were going on around us, perhaps it wasn't a bad performance by the team. To be honest, nothing was ever going to better our superb double in 1995–96, but it was nevertheless a very strange and sobering experience for me as a Bath captain not to have delivered any silverware back to the Rec last season. Make no mistake, we'll be back to teach our rivals a lesson in 1997–98!

With so many changes in the game itself, I was thrilled to be able to leave the England bench and start to play a meaningful role in the international side, and to do so as the new England captain was a wonderful honour. After much speculation, Jack Rowell told me that I was going to follow in Will Carling's footsteps while I was midway through a round of golf with some of the lads. It improved my golf that day – I sank a long putt moments after hearing from Jack on my mobile phone – and I think that the added responsibility has also helped sharpen my rugby, too.

As for the debate about which pairing should have played at centre in 1996–97, it's history. I think I earned my chance to play a full 80 minutes in the England jersey having waited a long time in the wings, and I believe the results spoke for themselves. England made a lot of progress in just a few games, and we played some really good, entertaining rugby. Will's attitude and performances were a credit to him throughout his last international season, and for Will and myself to have kept the world-class Jerry Guscott – perhaps the most gifted domestic footballer of all – on the bench was some going. But I've always been confident in my own sporting ability, and I've always known that I could make a telling contribution to the team, given the opportunity. Now I'm in the driving seat, and I won't be giving it up without a battle. I am determined to prove myself on the wider international stage, and my first season as England skipper has already gone some way towards achieving that goal.

The captaincy brings with it new personal pressures, and I reckon that it has toughened me mentally. As soon as I was appointed to the new job I talked about the role with Yolanda and we decided that, wherever possible, we would make a conscious effort to ensure that nothing would change our day-to-day lives and, ultimately, the way we behave. To date, nothing has . . . at least, not too drastically! We have come through unscathed, and both of us still manage to have a fairly relaxed attitude to life and all its riches.

Perhaps that's why I was only hurt rather than bitter about my omission from the British Lions squad to tour South Africa. Yes, perhaps it was a snub to me as the England captain not to have been picked for the squad, but, deep down, I felt the pain more as an outcast rugby player. I felt that I was good enough to tour on playing ability alone; the fact that I was the England captain had nothing to do with my reaction. And yet I suspected early on that I wouldn't make the cut: selection is always a subjective process, and never an easy one, and my limited contact with the tour manager Fran Cotton had been at ill-tempered affairs that were part of the RFU/EPRUC negotiations.

It's a shame that I didn't get my opportunity to play Lions' rugby. Ironically, I would have gone on the 1993 New Zealand tour as a late replacement had it not been for injury, despite at that time only being on the England bench. It can be a strange world.

I still have plenty of ambitions, of course, both on and off the field. But time waits for no man and I can already see the ripe old age of 30 on the horizon. Rugby today is a young man's game, and it's inevitable that sometimes I find myself thinking about the future. When my time with Bath is finally over, and family life takes over from the demands of English professional rugby, I hope to have the opportunity to play abroad for a while. With two years of my Bath contract still to run, it won't be yet. My heart and mind are still in the West Country. However, when the final whistle does blow for me in the 'Premiership', perhaps we'll think about a family move to play abroad, fitness permitting. If I've still got the enthusiasm, the energy and the turn of speed to make a break when it matters, it's something I'd like to try before those dirty boots are finally hung in the cupboard to gather dust.

PHIL DE GLANVILLE
MAY 1997

CHAPTER ONE

De Glanville Takes Centre Stage

'Fans who believe back-line attack and try-conscious rugby still have a place at semi-final time should venture to Ballymore tomorrow for the Colts grand finals. Wests are through to the big one in all three grades. Coach Stan Pilecki is most enthusiastic about the futures of several young bulldogs. He has a special word for centre Philip de Glanville, whose striking skills have led Pilecki to predict that the visiting teenager will play for his country.'

BRISBANE SUNDAY SUN, SEPTEMBER 1987

I was born in Loughborough on 1 October 1968, and christened Philip Ranulph de Glanville. It was a brave decision to bring me into the de Glanville squad, as my parents, Derek and Sue, were still students in their final year at Loughborough College.

But I was selected to make an appearance, and also given a sporting role in the new family team – even before I'd left the delivery room! No sooner had I been born than there was a pair of mini rugby boots at my side, an appropriate welcoming present for the young DG.

My mother didn't seem to mind; rugby was already playing an important part in her life, thanks to my father. I think mum really enjoyed the social side of the game which was just as well, because my father, Derek, played rugby for Loughborough, and also for Rosslyn Park. Although my mother was by no means sporty, my parents had a wide circle of sporting friends. It was always going to be like that at Loughborough, which is still well known for its sporting excellence.

Looking back, I admire them for the courage of their convictions. As students, it couldn't have been easy bringing me into the world, and I suspect that my folks came under a lot of pressure not to have me, but I still made my debut.

After graduation, the de Glanvilles left Loughborough for a two-year voluntary teaching post in Zambia. My sister Kieran was born out there, a little African baby. Her birthplace, Kashikishi, is always guaranteed to cause a stir when she shows her passport!

I don't have too many early memories of my time in Africa – and certainly none of playing any rugby, as I was still too young – but a couple of incidents do stick in my mind, and obviously made a deep impression. One is of a local catching, killing and skinning an adder, and the other is of my first serious tropical storm – just the sort of incident that would stay in the memory of a kid who was two or three years old. I remember one lightning strike during that huge storm as if it were yesterday. Fork lightning hit one of the trees in the back garden, some 15 metres away from where I was standing. It totally fazed me. The lightning stripped away the entire bark of the tree, and then travelled underground to our homemade steel swimming pool which lit up like a Christmas tree. I ran inside the house screaming, just as the electricity blew. There were sparks flying everywhere, so I hid under my bed and refused to come out. I was terrified. That's just one of a few 'near misses' I've had during my short life. As a teenager I had the misfortune to experience a terrorist attack in Cyprus, where my grandfather still lives. We were lucky to escape without injury. At least one innocent child was shot in a nearby boat when terrorists attacked the RAF Sailing Club with rockets, mortars and machine guns. We were in the way!

I was four years old when we returned to the UK from Africa. Mum and dad landed teaching jobs at Elmbridge School in Surrey, and we lived in the grounds. Mum taught maths, and my father PE and English. My only vivid memories are of fighting with my sister; she's still very competitive even now we are grown up and very close to each other.

Two years later we moved again, this time to Dulwich in south London where dad taught at Dulwich College and mum at Dulwich

College Prep. It was around that time that I began to play a little rugby. To be honest, I wasn't pushed into playing any particular sport when I was small, but I can remember throwing a rugby ball around with my father. Indeed, it wasn't until I left school that I had any inkling that rugby was 'my game'.

We moved to Devon when I was 11 years old, and I spent two years at Mount House Prep School in Tavistock. Then, at 13, I went to board at Bryanston School. After a few more years of teaching my father set up Rhino, a company with its heart, mind and business in the world of rugby and now well known for its scrummage machines and other rugby products. At the time it was a somewhat risky venture, and it marked a massive change of lifestyle for my father. He went into business with his brother-in-law who was based in north Devon, well over an hour away, so he had to start commuting and staying away from home two days a week. It was hard work at the start, and there was a lot of investment made in the initial scrummaging machine.

While dad was working hard on the baby Rhino, life for me at Bryanston was a revelation. One of the greatest things about going to a school like that was the opportunity to play sport in the superb 500-acre grounds, and lots of it: hockey and sevens in the spring, rugby in the winter and cricket in the summer. I also took up rowing in the first year, and got the opportunity to try my hand at shooting. The only sport not on the Bryanston play list was soccer.

It was an excellent grounding, and prepared me really well for university. Initially there were very few free lessons, but in the last year at school there were only one or two formal lessons every day, plus assignments with strict deadlines, with a tutor system in place to try and keep you on the straight and narrow – just the sort of lifestyle you are thrown into at university. It was good for the growing de Glanville as it allowed me to organise myself in my own time and at my own pace. In fact, the whole Bryanston system suited me and the way I learn. It must have worked well from both sides, because senior masters at the school have said kind things about me too. When I became England captain a former housemaster Peter Harvey told the press: 'Phil was entirely amiable, very reliable and strong in character. He is still a very modest and extremely pleasant chap who comes back to see us regularly.' I always did like him!

During my five years at Bryanston I played rugby for Devon Schools and also had junior-level trials for the South-west. In the holidays I played for Tavistock Colts, gradually progressing up to the heady heights of the first team. As a junior I played at scrum-half, not at centre. I was quite slight in build as a young teenager, although I'm told that my tackling was ferocious, with tackles being made 'as though my life depended on them'. But it wasn't until I left school that my rugby really began to develop, and a huge part of that development must be attributed to the sunshine and hard ground of Australia, where I spent one very happy rugby season learning more about the tools of my trade before going up to Durham University.

I took 'A' levels in English, history and economics at Bryanston along with two 'S' levels, and in my sixth form I twice applied to get into Oxbridge, specifically into Trinity College, Oxford and Queens. In my fourth term I applied to take economics and history, and I reached the interview stage, but fell down on my economics. Then I reapplied, having gained two As and one B in my 'A' levels, plus some commendable 'S' levels. It wasn't good enough! I would have to wait a few more years for my chance to break into Oxbridge, which was to come only thanks to my rugby skills.

Although I missed out on an Oxbridge place at that time I wasn't disheartened, as I'd already done well enough to secure a place at the beautiful University of Durham. I remember seeing Durham for the first time on the way to my university interview. When we crossed the viaduct by train I saw the amazing view of the snow-topped cathedral and castle. The magical view made a deep impression, and I sensed that Durham was the place for me. I still have many fond memories of the place, where I studied politics and economics, and I even managed a very respectable Bachelor of Arts degree with a grade 2:1 (despite my hatred of the increasing amount of maths in the economics!).

My big rugby breakthrough came at the university, although I have no doubt that much of my success was down to the Australian trip in my 'year off'. After leaving school I took time out so that I could go to Oz with the specific intention of playing rugby. Close friends of my father reckoned that they could help me get into a club over there, and the thought of playing in the southern hemisphere sun whetted my sporting appetite.

So, with the promise of some Aussie club rugby I set about earning my fare. I worked for Rhino, the family business, for about three months, and also on a building site; in fact, I worked anywhere I could to earn enough money to make the trip. Physically I had been quite small until the age of 16, but then I shot up and started to fill out, and the hard graft I put in during these few months must also have helped to beef me up a bit in readiness for my trip.

I flew to Australia on my own, arriving on New Year's Day 1987. First of all I back-packed to Sydney and stayed in a hostel, surviving on the equivalent of £2 per day! Then, in February, I moved on to Brisbane for the start of the rugby season, where I was booked in to stay with Dave Clarke, one of the technical directors of rugby for Queensland Rugby Union. I trained with Western Districts, Wests, and played in the colts team with a great bunch of guys. They gave me a warm welcome, and we blended together well. It proved an instant success. Nine of the boys in the team ended up playing for Queensland Colts that season. The other six of us, myself included, got the chance to play for Brisbane Colts.

I really came on as a player in those six months. The firm dry ground helped, and so did getting the ball all the time, and I proved a hit with my strong running and good handling skills. It meant that I was forced to make decisions, and yet more decisions, and physically I'd reached a stage where I could cope with the demands being made of me. All of a sudden, I began to find the game completely different. The impact of that year really was fundamental to my future rugby career, and, among other things, it saw me change position from scrum-half to centre, at the suggestion of my father. He felt I was getting too big to play at scrum-half, so I moved to centre shortly before I set off to Australia, and played in that position for Wests. It was a good call.

When I arrived in Durham in 1987, sounding like an Australian, Ted Wood was the student chairman of selectors and Durham coach. Thanks to my efforts in Oz, I moved straight into the university's first XV, playing alongside a younger but no less talented Will Carling, then in the driving seat as the dimple-chinned full-back for our important inter-university University Athletic Union (UAU) games. In my first Durham season, 1987–88, we reached the UAU semi-finals before being knocked out 22–0 by Swansea.

Will was a star when I came on the Durham rugby scene. He was already playing for Harlequins and made his full international debut for England during my first rugby season at university, an extraordinary achievement. By his own admission Will didn't actually do much academic work at university; it certainly seemed to me that he spent an awful lot of time in London playing for Quins. At that time he came across as being somewhat arrogant, but in retrospect I think that a lot of it could be attributed to his natural shyness. He was treated differently because of who he was and what he had done, and he treated us differently too. He didn't come out drinking, and he wasn't quite 'one of the boys'. I only really got to know him because I was part of the same rugby team, and even then it was not a close relationship. I knew him from afar. His mind was clearly on other things, and understandably so.

One freezing cold day, during the winter term of that 1987–1988 season, Ted Wood took me aside and told me that he had put me forward for an England 'A' team student trial the following week. I reacted to the news with a dismal display for the university that afternoon, my worst game of the entire season. The 'A' trial was held at St Paul and St Mary's, Cheltenham, where my performance improved markedly – it could not have got any worse – but I didn't get picked for the team. However, I did not have to wait long for my next chance. I was selected to play for England in the Student World Cup in the south of France in the summer of 1988. This was something of a surprise and a great thrill. My Bath teammate Victor Ubogu was also in that squad.

Before making the tour my parents took me on holiday to Portugal where I trained like a madman – I've probably never trained as hard as that – and it prepared me well. Our crazy team coach made us train in the unbearable French heat twice a day, every day, for one to two hours at a time. I remember that we even trained on the morning of games. I didn't play in the early rounds of the competition, which was very frustrating, but then I was called on from the bench in the game against New Zealand and scored a try. After that I was picked for the following game against Italy, where I won my first full international cap of any kind. It was a good game, and we won by 40-odd points. We eventually ended up playing Wales in the fifth and sixth place play-off, a match which I remember well because it took place in searing heat, 97 degrees Farenheit. Somehow we managed to withstand the temperature and still win convincingly.

It was a great experience and I returned to Durham with a reputation as being something of an 'international rugby star' – at least, that's what I told the girls! I began to get regular games for the England Students and recall playing against the Australians, when a young David Campese played an instrumental role in our 36–13 defeat.

During the 1988–89 season I received an invitation from Bob Reeves to try my hand in the senior team at Bristol RFC in the holidays. I played one game for Bristol seconds against Clifton RFC on Boxing Day 1988, and shortly afterwards one of the Bath coaches, Dave Robson, phoned me up. He must have been watching the game because he said, 'I think you'll play for England – come and play for Bath!' That was good enough for me, and just a few days later I made my debut for Bath seconds against Cardiff. There was no comparison between the two experiences, and the rest, I suppose, is detailed in Bath's club history. For me, that move to Bath was probably the biggest breakthrough of all. Although I was only playing for the seconds and thirds during the university holidays, it threw me into top-class rugby and I began to train and play with quality players on a regular basis.

In March 1989 this experience helped me to gain England 'B' honours against Italy in a 44–0 victory. It was one of Jerry Guscott's first games for the 'B' team, and I came on as a replacement. Two months later I scored two tries in the inaugural England Under-21 match against Romania in Bucharest, a game we won 54–13. In

April of that year I made my Bath first-team debut, against Newport at the Rec.

During 1989–90, my final rugby season (and last academic year) at Durham, I was playing for Bath seconds during the holidays, when I was at home in Devon, and for Durham City and Durham County as well as the university during term-time. I had made my debut for Durham in the local derby clash with Northumberland in January 1988. We reached the County final in 1989–90, and I was victorious at Twickenham for the first time.

I played some really hard games for Durham County, particularly against teams like Northumberland. I was only 20 years old and I came up against some huge, strong centres, who were prepared to tackle all day long. It wasn't a place for the faint-hearted, and, more often than not, it was pretty fierce. It may be some time ago, but I haven't forgotten some of those bone-crunching tackles.

Once my university days at Durham drew to a close, I was offered the chance to study at Oxford thanks to my rugby skills (skills which also gave me the chance to go on Bath's Australian tour that summer). Indeed, Oxford approached me with the opportunity to take a postgraduate course in social studies – ironic, seeing as I hadn't been able to get in as an undergraduate on the basis of my academic skills on either of the two occasions I had tried my hand.

My decision to go to St Catherine's, Oxford, in 1990 probably upset one or two people. During the summer of my second year at Durham I got the chance to travel to the Lisbon Sevens in Portugal with the Cambridge Past and Present rugby team, and we won the tournament. How did I manage that? Well, connections I suppose. Tony Rogers was the Cambridge coach, and he knew my dad very well. In the end I could have chosen Cambridge to continue my studies and my sport, but when I was given the choice, I didn't want to study land economy, the traditional course taken by rugby jocks. I reckoned that land economy wasn't going to take me anywhere, whereas the social studies course at Oxford included politics, economics and sociology, subjects that I had taken at Durham and wanted to pursue further. It may seem strange, I suppose. Rugby was the only reason I eventually gained entry to Oxbridge, and then I had the pick of either Oxford or Cambridge, yet the only reason I chose Oxford was for the academic course itself! Looking back, I have absolutely no regrets. It was a great time and I am very proud of what I achieved.

I often think about the interviews for Oxford and Cambridge and how little there is to choose between the candidates. It's not unlike international rugby, where there is so little to choose between so many good players. At the end of the day it often goes on the personal whims of the 'selector' and you never really know what they're after. For example, you don't know what admittance restrictions they have imposed on them in terms of the ratio of men to women, or, for that matter, the amount of talented sportsmen and women they can sneak through. No doubt these things come into play, and it means that, whatever you do, you are not in total control of your own destiny. It's just like being selected (or not) for England or the British Lions. It's not a black and white decision. You may think you're the best, but the selectors might well disagree.

I moved from the cathedral city of Durham to the ancient university city of Oxford and sank myself into all aspects of rugby. Before I went up to Oxford the known – earmarked – rugby players, mainly postgraduates, were thrown together for a pre-season tour to the Far East. We'd never met before, and firm friendships were quickly established in that melting pot.

I was awarded my precious 'Blue' playing for Oxford University against Cambridge in the 1990 Varsity Match at Twickenham. It was a unique occasion, and unless you've trained for and played in that game you can't understand the unbelievable pressure. We wedged a great many games into that intense Oxford season, playing against a lot of top-quality opposition every Wednesday and Saturday, but everything was ultimately geared towards the Varsity Match. The rugby against other teams was merely a means to one very specific end.

With everything focused on winning at Twickenham, the pressure began to mount early in the university term. By the end of my first term, shortly before the pre-Christmas game, things were at fever pitch. So much so that in the week before the match, when it snowed so heavily that we were prevented from training, nerves were stretched to breaking-point. We were huge underdogs for the Bowring Bowl. Oxford had played steadily throughout the season, but not well enough to have the edge on our skilful opposition, and Cambridge were very confident of success. But on the day it all went Oxford's way, every loose ball, every break, every refereeing decision. Even our unpredictable kicker Charlie Haly had a blinder.

As an experience it was unforgettable, but I expect that as a game it was a bore for the neutrals in the crowd. The play was scrappy and unmemorable, and it was all done at a frenetic pace. There was no time for skill, or shape, and no one talented player imposed himself on the drab affair; all of the hyped-up students on the field were running around like headless chickens! But it was a great occasion, and the party afterwards was superb.

As soon as my student days were over, club rugby dominated my agenda and I went to live in, and play for, Bath. I immediately found myself in the first team. I moved into the side as the replacement for the retiring Bath and England centre Simon Halliday, and went straight in as first choice centre partner to Jerry Guscott – quite a thrill! In many ways I'm not unlike Simon, hammering at the gain line on the field but unthreatening and sometimes even affable off it! He was also an Oxbridge Blue, so little changed when I took over. In fact, all the stick that he used to get simply transferred over to me.

The rugby experience was great, but when I left Oxford in 1991 I needed a proper job. Rugby was, after all, still an amateur game. Around that time, Leicester RFC asked me to join them, and I even went to a couple of job interviews in the Midlands which the club had arranged on my behalf. I could have very easily jumped ships and joined Leicester because they were giving me a lot of attention and 'TLC'; certainly more than I was getting from Bath. However, deep down I didn't really want to go to play for the Tigers.

I had a number of university 'milk round' interviews in London, including one with Unilever, but time and time again the issue of rugby and my heavy commitment to it crept up during the discussions. All of the companies I met were worried about how much time off I might need, and nobody was very supportive. All of that was to change after Jack Rowell put me in touch with two good recruitment consultants in the Bath area, David Dodd and Keith Townrow. David found me my first proper job, at Cow and Gate. I had an interview with the company, and was consequently offered a graduate traineeship in sales and marketing based in Trowbridge, which is not very far from Bath. I started work with Cow and Gate in September 1991.

I had met Yolanda, the woman who was later to become my wife, at Durham in my second year. She was also at the university, studying natural sciences. When I went to Oxford, Yolanda was in her final year at Durham, so we spent a lot of time commuting to see each other, and even more time on the phone. It was all pretty desperate, and I really didn't enjoy that part of the experience. I also made the mistake of living in a hall of residence in Oxford. Having spent my final year in Durham in a house with three friends, it was probably an error of judgement to live in a single room in hall, particularly as I wasn't too immersed in the day-to-day university life and therefore getting to know other students; I was travelling backwards and forwards either to Durham or to Bath. Postgraduates are also treated slightly differently by the undergraduates, probably because they don't get plastered in the bar every Saturday night. Is that being boring or just being more grown up . . .?

At the end of that final academic year, Yolanda and I packed our bags and went on what was supposed to be the holiday of a lifetime, but it ended up as a month-long holiday from hell. We went to Kenya and Egypt, and *en route* we both had chronic food poisoning, with all of the horrors it entails. Both of us had serious stomach upsets as a result during our stay in Kenya, which made our safari trip rather less than enjoyable, and then our passports, jab documents, traveller's cheques and money were stolen.

Everything was nevertheless going to work out okay, we thought, because friends of ours – seemingly a happy couple – were meeting us at Cairo Airport. They would bring money and comfort. We waited a whole day, but they never arrived (it transpired they had split up and decided not to travel, without letting us know!). If it hadn't been for a generous Israeli husband and wife who lent us £150, we'd probably still be in the airport. It was the ultimate test for Yolanda and myself and, after two years together, we came through. We reckoned that if we could make it through a trip like that, we could make it through anything.

Once Yolanda had completed her degree at Durham she went on to Cambridge to undertake a PGCE. 'Trowbridge to Cambridge,' I thought. 'Not too bad.' But I didn't marry my long-term sweetheart until July 1995, when we tied the knot at the magnificent King's College Chapel in Cambridge, where Yolanda's father is a fellow.

I began working at Cow and Gate in September as planned, but it was hard work without a car. For the first six months I had to hitch a lift into work from anyone and everyone who travelled in from Bath, and that was a pain. I relied massively on the generosity of Neil Watkins and Richard Hall, who have since become demon three-card brag players and good friends! But work was enjoyable. I spent the first six months in the marketing department, then another six months in sales under the wing of the marketing director as the company had no formal graduate training programme.

The people at Cow and Gate were very supportive in all respects. Even when I began work there was a delicate balance to be struck between my career and rugby, and every year it became more and more difficult as I progressed as a player, and the demands of the game started to become ever greater. During the first year, all I needed was time off for the summer tour. Apart from that I worked a normal five-day week. In the second year it suddenly became a tour plus a couple of days off before internationals. It rapidly became more and more awkward, and had it not been for the company generously allowing me unpaid leave (and a great deal more) it would have been impossible. Other players, particularly the self-employed, found it very difficult indeed.

In those early playing days I found the rugby itself very challenging, not necessarily physically but mentally. It wasn't just turning out in the bodily sense that was so demanding. You needed to be up to it mentally as well. I found a lot of caustic dressing-room banter, like there is at any rugby club, but at Bath it was pretty fierce. And there were a lot of challenges being laid down by teammates to prove yourself on the pitch, and a huge amount of peer pressure was continually being brought to bear. For instance, I remember Eric Peters first joining the club. He used to get kicked to bits by John Hall, Andy Robinson and Ben Clarke. It was just one of the hurdles you had to leap if you were going to be accepted by your teammates. They were a pretty tough bunch; they still are. It's a demanding and challenging atmosphere where a wide range of characters are thrown together by the overwhelming desire to be winners. You are forced to stand up and fight your corner. There are no hiding places.

I learned a lot from people like Stuart Barnes in those early days, and pretty quickly too. We had a number of other very experienced players in the team at the time, including scrum-half Richard Hill and my fellow centre and partner in crime Jerry Guscott, who was already coming into his prime.

CHAPTER TWO

Rugby in the Melting Pot

Yes, it is a whole new ball game. Professionalism has already changed every aspect of the sport, but the changes were forced on us far too quickly and the game has suffered as a result. This is despite the so-called moratorium for the first season imposed by the RFU, which quickly came to emphasise the deep division between clubs and administration. Cracks soon began to show, and those cracks quickly widened.

It has always been assumed that money has been the only major issue, and there is no question that money, in one form or another, has had huge and far-reaching effects on the way things have developed. But when players are training or running onto the field, they are not thinking about the cash. Professionalism brought with it other, less obvious, demands. It's not just about being paid to play. As far as the individual is concerned professionalism should be as much about a businesslike approach to the game as it is about cash. It's a state of mind, and it has already become evident that some players are not up to the new self-discipline it requires. Indeed, many clubs have also fallen well short of the new administrative demands imposed by the professional game. But professional rugby union could have been so different, and it very nearly was.

Some of the key England players were already pushing for more recognition, and more rewards, in 1994 and earlier. Rob Andrew and Brian Moore had been at the forefront of these moves. They argued that international players should at least get some reasonable compensation for loss of earnings, even if they weren't officially being paid for the huge amount of time and effort being put into training, travelling on tours and playing – although that was certainly on the agenda too. And these negotiations were on behalf of everyone playing international rugby, whether they were playing at senior, 'A' or Under-21 level. Once you get to this stage everyone puts in roughly the same amount of time, commitment and effort, and that commitment had been increasing with every season that went by. Something had to give.

That fact hit home when we toured South Africa in 1994. The players, and the England management and administrators, saw first hand what was happening. The South Africans were effectively being paid. They were full-time professional rugby players, who were able to train during the day. It was an accepted way of life over there. At last some of the key administrators saw the reality of what we had been telling them for years.

What did they do? In truth, nothing much, although they must have returned from South Africa knowing that things had to change. However, very little did until the International Rugby Football Board (IRB) threw the game open in August 1995, taking everybody by surprise – including the guys who had been recommending that the game here 'prepare itself' in readiness for professionalism. The players, administrators and even journalists were stunned.

It was a momentous decision, and one which drove a wedge between England's top clubs and the RFU. The move from an amateur code to an 'open game' happened too quickly. In the end, it came as too much of a surprise, throwing everything and everyone – including the RFU itself – into total confusion. It caused a truck-load of problems, many of which could probably have been avoided by employing a little time for thought and pre-planning.

When Bath RFC and the other senior clubs took in the news about the new 'open' structure of the game that autumn, rugby was effectively in chaos. Nobody quite knew what to do first – and nobody knew where the money was going to come from to do it. The RFU chose to tread water on 'open' rugby for a while, and declared a moratorium until the end of the 1995–96 season, during which time a 'status quo' needed to be maintained. But the senior clubs rightly felt that they needed to act swiftly, and they formed

English First Division Rugby Ltd (EFDR) the forerunner of EPRUC, to act as a safeguard and ensure a profitable future. The immediate financial demands of EFDR created the first of many stand-offs between the clubs and the RFU.

It was an anxious period. At first glance, all the media talk of professionalism and the open game painted a very rosy picture of the future to the supporters and even to the players. The fans were already raising their expectations of what they would see on the pitch. And some top players – including our own Mike Catt – were soon so confident of the future that they took the brave decision to turn pro, without hesitation and without the comfort of the fall-back position of a signed club contract. But these expectations were only castles built on the sand until the men with real money started to take an interest in rugby union. Without a few fat cheque-books and the hope of an agreement with the RFU, there was little or no finance available to pay players and to sort out an administrative, planning and managerial structure within the clubs to support professionalism.

It was during this period of uncertainty that wealthy and opportunistic entrepreneurs such as Sir John Hall and Ashley Levett turned their attentions to the new business of rugby by stepping in at Newcastle and Richmond respectively. At Bath we still had our 27-man committee, who were doing little, if anything, to react to the new demands and opportunities of professionalism. It was hopeless. I went to committee meeting after committee meeting to report that we were going to lose talented players unless they moved quickly. But 'quickly' was not a word in rugby's amateur club committee vocabulary, and by January 1996 offers were flooding in for some of our best players from clubs who had begun to get their acts together – in particular Richmond RFC. Richmond get the lion's share of the blame for the now excessive club wage bills which may threaten the viability of many of our most famous clubs.

If it hadn't been for Richmond making such extraordinary financial offers – and I saw some of them – there wouldn't be such high wage bills in the senior game today, demands which are putting unnecessary pressure on what are still generally limited resources.

Richmond would use 'market forces' to justify their cavalier approach. But if the game had planned in advance to go professional, and taken the step in a sensible time frame, there could have been rules on hot topics such as capping wages.

There was no question that Bath panicked during this period, as we set about trying to find large investors, and thank heavens for greetings card entrepreneur Andrew Brownsword – not a rugby fan as such, but a proven successful businessman and a Bath man through and through. Brownsword allowed Bath the funds to keep some of our leading players. We might not have matched the crazy offers made by other clubs, but the promise of guaranteed League One rugby certainly helped swing a few arguments. We also took the opportunity to point out that any top player moving to a smaller, less competitive club might well lose his international place. One way or another we generally held sway. However, a lot of that spiralling wage chaos might well have been avoided had Richmond not blown the market sky high in an effort to lure players away from First Division clubs.

It was also into this rugby 'void' that the plans for a World Rugby Corporation (WRC) so nearly bore fruit, long before the Rugby Football Union began their protracted battle with the organisation representing the clubs, EPRUC. Had it not been for the South Africans pulling out of the WRC at the very last moment, the UK – indeed, the world – club game would now be completely different. All, and I mean all, of the world's top players were ready to be involved.

Ross Turnbull first came to the UK to talk about the WRC in the autumn of 1995, after the Rugby World Cup in South Africa and around the time of the IRB announcement about the brave new world of open rugby. Ross had his cheque-book in hand, and a wedge of cash from global media magnate Kerry Packer. Brian Moore telephoned me and said that Ross was coming over to see me with 'a few ideas'. He came down to Cow and Gate and I met him one to one. Ross told me that 'the unions would keep pissing us around' and that the players would not get what we deserved, adding, 'We think international capped players deserve £200,000 per year, and 'A' capped internationals £150,000.'

How do you think I reacted? Pretty much the same as the rest of the boys, I can tell you.

Ross went on to tell me that the New Zealanders and South Africans were 'already on board' and that he had made 'signing-on' payments, with the funds put up by mega-wealthy Kerry Packer. The WRC, he claimed, was going to work. The new WRC playing structure was going to be based around regional franchises, one in the South-west, one in the South-east, one in the North and so on, and all the best players in those franchised divisions would play together against other franchised areas. Where we eventually ended up playing would depend on who purchased the franchise, and that could have been anyone and anywhere. I am certain that the South-west team would have ended up in Bristol, for instance, although as far as I was concerned that would have counted against the idea! There would have been international games as well, a northern and southern hemisphere equivalent of the Super 10s.

The WRC had already expended plenty of effort planning the southern hemisphere set-up and getting it ready, but there was also a blueprint for a northern hemisphere competition where sides from England, Scotland, Ireland, Wales, France and Italy would all play each other in leagues and play-offs. It would be a truly international tournament involving the professional players in all of those areas.

We had numerous meetings, and Ross visited Bath again to meet all the local players in the area. There were a lot of questions to begin with, and David Powell, our players' solicitor, checked the man out. After much debate we agreed to sign the contracts *only* if they were held in readiness for both the green light from Kerry Packer, his backer, which would release all the funds to make the project a runner and, of course, the commitment from the TV companies, which would ultimately make the WRC a winning concept.

The players were as one, ready to go. We had the majority of the England squad and the England 'A' squad ready and waiting. The contracts were signed and held by David Powell, not to be released until our criteria were met. Those criteria included the money in the bank! By 1 January 1996 Ross had to have the franchises confirmed and the funds in place. If he had come up with the goods at that stage, we would now have been playing in his new competition under the WRC banner.

There is no question that the WRC had some ideas which were particularly appealing to the players. They were forward-thinking ideas which would have benefited the game then and would still be benefiting the game even now, nearly two years on. For example, it was proposed that there would be a team of fully professional referees, chosen by a group of players and management – a very sound idea.

The whole concept of the World Rugby Corporation initiative was well thought through, and the proposal was very professional in terms of how it would be run and how the competition would be structured. Perhaps the key thing was that the players were 'valued' – and I don't just mean in a monetary sense. In fact, I think we were well overvalued in terms of what he was offering us financially. However, he saw what the players were able to offer the well-being of the game itself, and he valued their contribution to the future running of the game and the developments being planned. That WRC willingness to involve the players and consult them about what would be best for the game gave us a sense of worth; it is something the RFU have never ever come close to achieving, or perhaps even considering.

While the clubs are now becoming a little more active in seeking players' advice and involvement in decision-making, there are many influential people in the RFU who continue to treat the players like pawns. Their approach has always been: 'Go and do your stuff, sit down, shut up and be a good boy.' The startlingly different approach of the WRC was liked and appreciated by all the players, and, set alongside the absolutely massive financial incentive, it struck us as the right way to go. And once we had signed we really thought it was going to happen.

It was a crazy, mixed-up time. We had WRC meetings at the Compleat Angler hotel in Marlow, where the England team stays before internationals and close to where it regularly trains at Bisham

Abbey. In fact, we actually signed the WRC contracts at the hotel one Wednesday night prior to an England training session. The whole squad signed as one, almost being whipped away to the WRC right from under the noses of the RFU! We had in fact agreed to sign the contracts at an earlier meeting held at the Compleat Angler, but it transpired that the RFU had got wind of a 'secret players' meeting'. We were suddenly told that 'they' were in the hotel, and everyone darted out the back door and ran away! It was bizarre.

I understand that there had even been cross-conferencing between the big international southern hemisphere teams, where the New Zealanders, South Africans and Australians had all chatted to one another. And, by that stage, all of them had signed the deal. The WRC were down to the final negotiations with some of the home countries, when the South Africans pulled out. I don't know the ins and outs of why or exactly how it happened, but the captain François Pienaar did some kind of a bumper financial deal with South Africa's dictatorial rugby union president Louis Luyt. It must have involved huge sums of money. The gamble bought them out of the WRC contract, and without the key players from the world champions and one of the biggest teams in the world game in terms of fanatical support, the WRC plans collapsed like a pack of cards. Afterwards, Ross came back and tried again, but his credibility had been blown. Soon after, the ringmaster Kerry Packer withdrew his backing.

That window of opportunity for the WRC won't open again, but there were plenty of good ideas on how to run the game which could still be introduced to the benefit of rugby. There was an enormous amount of confusion when the game had been thrown open in August 1995, and the WRC plans only added to the chaos. When it was very close to happening, before the turn of the year, the RFU told the England players that they would make a generous counter offer. After the WRC collapsed those sums were suddenly, and very conveniently, forgotten! No surprise there. But in many ways the RFU missed a huge opportunity at that time – one of many it has missed and continues to miss. If it had moved in and contracted all the top players at that stage, the RFU wouldn't have had the drawn-out battle that it has had with the senior clubs. It would have been game, set and match. As it was, the RFU didn't get itself together, and we eventually ended up signing contracts with our league clubs.

Nobody should have been surprised that the RFU missed the golden opportunity to tie the players in to the way it wanted to run the game, even though there were one or two people internally who knew that that was what it should have been doing. But, although the idea was probably floated, the committees took the age-old approach to player relations: 'Pay players? No way.'

In the long term it would have worked out cheaper for the RFU if it had seen the opportunity more clearly, together with the danger of not making a positive move. When EPRUC and the other home club associations were formed during the summer of 1996 the battle lines were drawn afresh, moving the focus away from the already faded threat of the WRC and shifting it back again on to the already serious and growing division between the RFU and the senior clubs. Instead of Turnbull's WRC against the RFU, all eyes were now fixed intently on the clash between the clubs and the RFU.

There were some stories flying about that a few of the top clubs were considering getting together and forming a copycat, home-based WRC, or at least something similar to what Turnbull had been proposing. I am sure it was discussed, and it could have been close to happening, with four or five of the top teams breaking away. But, when push came to shove, I don't think that it was financially viable on this mini scale.

This is not the place for a history of the protracted wrangle between the clubs and the RFU, but it is important to know that relations were strained to breaking-point. The election of 'no-compromise' Cliff Brittle as chairman of the RFU executive in May 1996 (and, in one fell swoop, as chairman of the RFU's 'negotiating team') rapidly sent the situation hurtling towards the precipice. Brittle came with a 'mandate' from the grass-roots counties and refused to budge from his dogmatic position. It was only when RFU president Bill Bishop became more involved as a mediator that any progress began to be made.

Newcastle's Sir John Hall commented, 'I thought the word "niet" had gone out with the end of the Cold War. It hasn't. The RFU have reinvented it and have used it at every turn. You simply cannot carry on negotiations that way. The money required by the game to go professional won't go away.' It is alleged that Sir John Hall and Mr Brittle came close to fighting more than a war of words at one tense meeting.

Despite the obvious frustrations, EPRUC nevertheless continued to push hard for the right to secure the money it felt was necessary for the clubs to open the door to professionalism, while the RFU stood its ground, requiring 'ultimate control'.

Perhaps one of the key moments in all of the negotiations between EPRUC and the RFU was when EPRUC approached the England players and asked them to throw their weight behind their clubs. At that time I was drawn into the debate as one of the England team's spokesmen.

EPRUC wanted the England squad to sign side letters to our club contracts, allowing the clubs to control our every movement. If we did so they would have control over when we would be available for international training sessions and even for internationals and tours. If we signed it meant that EPRUC, the clubs, would have a crucial bargaining tool enabling them to turn the heat up on the RFU round the negotiating table.

Myself, Lawrence Dallaglio, Ben Clarke, Dean Richards and Damian Hopley talked to the squad about the issues, and EPRUC came to see us at the Hilton Hotel near Terminal 4 at London Heathrow. The new contract effectively signed away our international rights. There was a financial recompense for the risk the England squad would take, a minimum £40,000 'guaranteed', if we weren't able to play international rugby (or if EPRUC decided we were going to play in a different international competition to the Five Nations). There was a representative from almost every club at that meeting, including the big guns like Sir John Hall, Donald Kerr and Peter Wheeler.

The England players talked long and hard about the move in a debate which must have lasted about two hours. We talked about the perceived dangers of signing, the issues, and what the clubs were ultimately trying to do. Rather than making a play for control of the game, we felt that the clubs were simply trying to gain enough control to be able to ensure and protect their income streams, so critical in the new era of professionalism. They needed to be able to negotiate their own contracts for television deals and sponsorships, so that they would know how much income they were going to get. They didn't want it to be syphoned off and spent elsewhere, without their say-so. Basically, they argued for a greater control of their income stream so that they could run their businesses properly, and we all felt that that was fair enough. If the clubs did not have the ultimate control over their income streams and their finances were left in the hands of the RFU, the RFU committee would be able to decide how much money they were going to get. Without sufficient cash some of the clubs might have started going to the wall, unable to pay their players.

The key point for the England squad – the men forced into the middle – was that we felt we had to do everything we could to make sure that our own clubs were going to survive in the long term, because they paid not only our salaries, but also the salaries of all of the players in the First and Second Divisions – some 250 players all told. The 40-strong England squad could have swung the balance the other way if it had refused to co-operate with EPRUC. If the international players had just signed the £70,000 contracts with the RFU for the year, we would have been okay for that year, but we might not have had a professional club to go back to in the future. We couldn't stand on the touchline and watch our clubs put to the sword and jeopardised financially when we could do something that might help. The 'England 40' felt that there were another 210 players in the game who might suffer unless we supported the position of the clubs.

However, although the England squad signed the EPRUC side agreements, we agreed that they should only come into force if a certain percentage of other (non-international) players from the Courage League's Divisions One and Two signed them as well. Our biggest concern was that the RFU would tell the 40 rogue players that they were no longer required, and pick another squad to play for England. So, after that meeting, EPRUC dashed around all of the clubs getting players signed up. I've got a complete list of all the players who signed contracts, and it was the majority of English qualified players in the top two divisions. We needed to do that to guarantee that everybody would be in the same boat. The England players reckoned that if we were looking after the rest of the players, then they had to look after us by not playing for any makeshift England team.

In the end I think we acted in the best interests of all of the players, and that's what we kept as our overriding principle. It was nevertheless one hell of a panicky time, and very hectic when EPRUC was going round the clubs to get the other players' signatures. But we were kept fully informed, and that was the best thing about it. EPRUC were talking to us about what was going on in the negotiations with the RFU, while the RFU were not.

The £40,000 EPRUC sweetener to the players was laid down as a guarantee in case we had to form another international competition and in the event that we didn't end up playing for England. It was comforting to know that the money was in the background if things went wrong, but it wasn't really about the cash for us. In the final analysis, the players have actually had a split in terms of money: part from EPRUC (which replaced the retainer from the RFU) and match fees from the RFU, which we would have got anyway. It has actually worked out quite well and it is fair. In financial terms the England players are getting pretty much what we would have got from the RFU itself in the first place.

As I write, EPRUC and the RFU are working together much better. Relations are now a little more settled, and, for the most part, the people who are involved are good for the game. However, there are still important things to watch out for. It is already important, and it will become increasingly so, to try to strike a balance on the administration between the elements from within rugby and the businessmen. If we can do this, then I'm sure everything will be okay.

The relationship with the RFU has improved. The organisation is now treating the players a lot better, although communication is still poor. The RFU is already aware of this, but the players intend to keep on pointing it out until it is improved! I think I can safely say that talking to the players before it makes a decision is not the RFU's forte. For example, the RFU still refuses to talk to us about the structure of the 1997–98 season, something it really should do.

Of course, the RFU is made up of many different people, and, like any organisation, some are good and some are not. At least Tony Hallett and Colin Herridge from the RFU always tried to keep lines of communication open to the players. I know that Cliff Brittle is a reluctant supporter of the professional game, and I think he would have preferred the code to stay amateur. While some of his views are right and some are wrong, in my opinion his approach is generally quite extraordinary. He is very dictatorial, and treats the players as if they were schoolchildren.

Nobody would pretend that EPRUC was perfect either, and with barriers to progress on both sides it often made constructive talks very difficult. There were several occasions on which both sides were unwilling to enter a meeting and 'negotiate'.

The worst thing about the whole of last season – in fact, the last two seasons – was that the row between the RFU and the senior clubs continued to drag on for so long and the players were sucked into the battle. While all that was going on, the playing side of the game moved on in leaps and bounds in terms of fitness, training and tactical awareness. If we hadn't had the mess between the RFU and EPRUC continually hanging over our heads during that time, who knows how far we might have come on together?

There is no question that the RFU was at the very heart of the problem. The organisation was playing what it must have thought was a cunning waiting game, but I don't think the RFU ever fully appreciated the disruption it caused. It probably felt that EPRUC would run out of money and was prepared to wait until the body was on its knees, rather than taking a joint, and conciliatory, approach. That was a real shame. It would have been far better to say, 'Let's work together, and set up something which is good for the game as a whole.' But no way. I just could not understand the approach. Admittedly there were some idiots on the EPRUC side, with agendas other than the long-term future of the game. That may have been inevitable under the circumstances. But the RFU made it so much harder by not taking a more sensible considered approach which would have satisfied the majority of moderates. In doing so it managed to alienate those moderates in the senior clubs, leaving the door ajar for some of the more outspoken members to hold sway – people who were claiming that the RFU was intent on shafting the clubs because it was being so antagonistic. Thank goodness something gave, and we have been able to move on.

So how did rugby bosses handle the move to a new, 'open', professional game? In Alex Spink's *Rugby Union Who's Who 1996–97* he surveyed international players, and 65 per cent of us awarded them five out of ten or less for their efforts. I gave them two out of ten, Will Carling one out of ten, and Scott Hastings asked if he could award minus figures! But, despite the inept introduction of professionalism, it would seem that none of us wants to return to the way it was before.

While the RFU administrators and the senior clubs fought themselves to a virtual standstill over the control of the open, professional game and its finances, in Bath the stresses and strains of professionalism were also becoming all too evident throughout the 1996–97 season. Player power had swept John Hall into the job of director of rugby at the club some 18 months earlier. As well as being a long-serving and dedicated Bath club captain, John was a player's man, and that was his major strength. But the new professional game put such heavy demands on both the club and its officers that John was pulled away from the day-to-day needs (and training) of the guys on the pitch – the things he was good at – into the tedious and time-consuming world of rugby administration. It didn't work out and in early 1997 John was asked to go, a business decision made without reference to me as club captain, or any other players for that matter. The game on and off the pitch had clearly moved on.

CHAPTER THREE

Learning the New Business

Bath Rugby Football Club is now a business, not an amateur rugby club run by a committee. The committee members are still there, of course, and perform a valuable social function, as they do at the heart of any rugby club. But Bath is now run as a company, in a complete change of strategy and direction since just 18 months ago.

We defeated Wasps in the 1995 Pilkington Cup final, and I captained the team in John Hall's absence. This, his last game for the club after a distinguished career, was meant to be his final swansong, but injury kept him on the sideline at Twickenham that day. Although I was skipper, John rightly went up to collect the trophy after a comprehensive 36–16 victory.

We may have won the Cup, but, all told, it wasn't considered a very successful season by the exacting Bath standards. And it is true that things were not quite 'on song'. Jack Rowell had left the year before and his departure created a hole at the club which coach Brian Ashton was not strong enough to fill. Something of a power struggle ensued between the stronger characters involved in Bath rugby, including John Hall and Richard Hill. So, after the cup-final victory, the players set about putting the house in order. We decided that there was a straight choice between John and Richard for the position of the new Bath RFC supremo.

Richard Hill had retired, and he was doing some coaching. But as club captain that season John Hall (aka Hally) had done a commendable job to help shore up the gap in the absence of a strong guiding hand. Without any question the team and the club were entirely player-driven at that time, and we were therefore in a position to vote for Hally to take on the role. With one man in charge, we reckoned that there would be no more wrangling. We felt it would unite and better focus the club.

There have always been strong players with powerful ambitions on and off the pitch at Bath RFC. But, while players like Richard Hill and Hally may have gelled beautifully together on the field of play, off the field they didn't always get on too well. When I first joined Bath I don't remember any particular dressing-room tensions. I was too busy getting involved and trying to enhance my own playing career. But I was always aware of a little needle. That's why Richard Hill left the club and went to Gloucester after John Hall got the players' vote, and probably why Richard's pal Gareth Chilcott, another Bath great, followed him to our local rivals.

After the players' dressing-room decision I went to the Bath committee as the new skipper and said that we needed to find a way to pay John. They replied that it wasn't possible and, after a massive row, he had to take on the role for nothing (a situation which lasted for quite a while). Nevertheless, it worked out well in playing terms. Despite the game lurching from pillar to post off the pitch, our 1995–96 season, and my first full season as Bath captain, was highly successful and we won the League and Cup double. John Hall cleared up the management muddle. Hally was in there as the top man and had his own people, and he worked well with club coach Brian Ashton.

When John Hall was appointed, everyone was right behind him, and, in many ways, that's why it was such a shock when he was sacked earlier this year. It was only little more than a year and a half since the team had sat down and effectively chosen the top man, and then, suddenly, it was all change and we didn't have a say about who was the coach or who was the manager. It's all history now. As club captain I only found out that John had been asked to go shortly before the press. Player power had been consigned to 'Room 101' together with the influence of the captain, once the man who had taken all of the club's key decisions on the playing side.

It must have been very painful for Tony Swift to ask John to leave the club. It's always difficult for a player to move into either a coaching or a management role at the same club, because you know the players and colleagues as friends. Close friendships make the business side much harder, and it must have hurt to have to tell John that Andrew Brownsword 'no longer had enough confidence' in him, and that it would be better to go now rather than wait until the end of the season. It was a clear illustration, if one is needed, that today's rugby is all about business off the pitch as well as on it. However, although there is now a new businesslike attitude, club administration has often fallen short, particularly in terms of player support and personal management. The business side seemed to become distanced from the players just at the key time.

After the defeat against Leicester in the 1996–97 season the players sat and talked about the impact and implications of the new professional game. I know that a lot of players were, and probably still are, finding it difficult. Although we were always pushing for the day when we would be paid a fair wage, I don't think many people realised the full extent of what it actually involves. It wasn't just about deciding whether to make it a full-time job, although that in itself has caused some debate. In the Alex Spink *Rugby Union Who's Who* survey of international players, 41 per cent of us said that we didn't want to be full-time professional rugby players.

I think that some problems also arose because the new-found 'professional' status immediately put the onus on the players to organise their own lives, whereas in the past our days had been arranged for us into the neat 9 a.m to 5.30 p.m. working patterns and demands of normal business life. Initially our club training sessions were set in stone, and everything else, such as weights, was voluntary. It was left up to the players to turn up, on time, 'ready for the work of rugby' with the 'proper' professional attitude to fitness and training. But nobody explained exactly what was expected, and what that 'proper' attitude was. There were no guidelines issued, and no advice on how to organise your time effectively. Consequently it is not surprising that many players were unable to take that added responsibility on board themselves. Admittedly, some of them are still working, and I come into that category.

It struck me that there were a few players not attending the extra voluntary sessions simply because they were not disciplined enough to get there – particularly early on in the season. Before turning professional, when silverware was all we were playing for, we used to have a dozen or more guys at training at 7 a.m. Now we might only have seven turn up for a session at 2 p.m., and we're all being paid.

It's getting much better now, but there are still a few players who are struggling with the new demands of full-time rugby, particularly with the self-discipline it requires, and so far they have been unable to embrace the move to the professional era. The situation was made worse initially as the necessary club administration was not in place to help this new professional structure; until recently there was little or no man management in place to coax and encourage, advise and reprimand. Bath were much too slow in putting this into place, and had John Hall taken more decisive action in this respect, he would probably have made things easier for himself. Having said that, I'm not sure he had the resources at his disposal to provide effective back-up.

One of the first things that Clive Woodward, the former Leicester and England centre and Bath's new tracksuited backs coach, said when he came to the club was that being professional is not just about being paid. It's true, or should be. You don't think about money when you are training or playing; you're still doing what you have always done, only doing it more often and getting paid in the process. Professionalism should be an attitude of mind in rugby as it is in business. It's about turning up for work smartly dressed, as you would for work in a business environment. You don't turn up shabbily dressed. You are part of a team. It's about being on time for training, and being even earlier if you have got to get strapped up. It's about fulfilling your obligations to the sponsors, and making sure you are wearing the appropriate clothes.

At Bath there were people going through these fundamental changes in lifestyle, and some of them were not coping. It was only to be expected. To be professional they needed to apply themselves, but for one reason or another couldn't do so. And for the most part there was nobody around to help them through the change. It was a new world for Bath rugby, but there were still a couple of players messing around in training, or turning up late. But you couldn't do that any more. To some extent that's where Hally fell down, because he wasn't hard enough on the guys who had fallen behind. He should have been tougher on the offenders and fined them.

But I reckon the biggest mistake Hally made was in failing to play to his real rugby strength: he wasn't managing the players any more. Instead he'd been pulled into the management of the club. He was sucked into buying new players and into day-to-day administration because he didn't have the back-up he needed to run the club in the new era. He ended up dealing with registrations, signing off invoices and sorting out expenses, none of which were 'his bag'. Hally was literally managing the club and he left the players to it, when those same players should have come first in terms of management time and resource. That's where the hole was in the first part of the 1996–97 season, and probably why Bath were unsuccessful during that sometimes harrowing campaign. There was plenty of talent around but it wasn't being managed in a way that would maximise its undoubted potential.

It didn't help that I was unable to take on more of that player-management role as club captain. I probably did less than I had the season before, because in the new professional game I was just another player as far as the club was concerned, especially in my second term in the role. To some extent professionalism has diminished the role of club captain. When John was skipper he had the final say in selection, and in many other areas of our rugby lives. If he didn't want us to train one night, we didn't train. If he wanted us to go somewhere else rather than the Rec, for one reason or another, we went there. Hally had the final say; he was all-powerful. I took over that mantle of captaincy in the 1995–96 season, and then I was 'the man'. But during the 1996–97 season that changed completely. A captain is no longer the circus ringmaster that he once was. I used to have to tell people that they were dropped, and was required to be able to justify the decision. Now I contribute to matters of selection, but I don't have the final say, just an input. And I certainly don't have the influence and control that John had as a skipper in the amateur days. It's not like that any more, and it won't be like it again. The captain is another player, and he cannot be allowed to be the sole arbiter of things like weekly team selection because now that has a direct link to players' salaries.

Nevertheless, I think all of us at Bath RFC recognised that we were missing someone taking direct personal responsibility for the players, someone to show an interest and to individually man manage, a role that oddly enough used to be much more prevalent in the old amateur days. There was nobody around on whom a player could lean, someone who could and would take you aside and say, 'Your kicking isn't good enough, come with me' or 'What's happening in your life? What's affecting your game? Let's sit down and talk about it.'

Hally should have made that man-management job his top priority. Brian Ashton used to pick off bits and pieces of this role, but in the 'absence' of John, who was in the office, Brian definitely wasn't the man to take over that bigger man-management role, even though he may have thought that he was. He simply wasn't tough enough. I have a huge respect for Brian Ashton, he's a fantastic bloke and a great coach, but he was never a great man manager. Brian ultimately wanted to manage things at the club that he wasn't equipped to handle, and he left partly because of that.

As a school and a training ground for life, Bryanston was great for me because I was told what I needed to do and where the books were to help, and then I went away and got on with it. Other kids needed a more structured approach with more formal lessons and teaching because they had to have that support mechanism in order to learn and progress. The same is currently true in professional rugby. It's not good enough to tell some players that the club is putting on a session at a certain time and they can attend if they wish. The best approach for them has got to be: 'You will be at this place, at this time. Don't miss it, and don't be late.' This is certainly the approach the club takes now.

The other key element that was initially lacking in this new era of professionalism at Bath RFC was regular skill development, again partly due to the absence of that player supremo who would coax and cajole the very best from you week in, week out. Professionalism should give you more time to work on fitness and skills, but Bath did not spend enough time working on skills during the 1996–97 season. Generally players worked hard on fitness, and even harder on technical training. But there was not enough emphasis on skill development, especially during the early part of the season. That is part of the personal management of an individual player in terms of identifying and analysing weaknesses and working to improve them. Admittedly it's a massive job with a squad of 30 players. But we were six months into the season before we began having regular player reviews; it was too late to make a real difference.

This is yet another illustration of the administration playing catch-up with all of the other developments in the game following August 1995. At club level there was a lack of understanding about what was required in terms of back-up and administration. In many respects it has also been the same at England level. You need a skilled support team in the background to help make things work on the pitch, and some key people have only just realised this. One big advantage that the Lions squad had on the tour to South Africa was the presence of some of the best administrators around, and one of the best support teams possible. That was Fran Cotton doing his job professionally, and all credit to him for his foresight.

Since turning professional my career and my lifestyle have changed significantly, as have the careers and lifestyles of all my teammates. I had moved on to a four-day working week at Cow and Gate in the early months of 1995, which freed up two mornings a week for training and everything else that I needed to do to get me 100 per cent match fit and ready for a big game. Shortly before the new rugby season began in 1995 the game was 'opened up', and before too long I moved jobs with a contract that only required me to work three days per week. It was a career move which gave me a much greater degree of flexibility.

By then I had started spending what was effectively a whole day at home during the week. I went to training in the morning, came home, then went to training again in the afternoon. But once our new Bath contracts were signed in August 1996, the training regime changed and we were thrown into daytime training on Mondays and Tuesdays, a heavy commitment which is now forcing players to choose between full-time employment and the game. Working my three-day week immediately became harder, and that quickly became two days a week. Since I took on the England captaincy in November 1996 I am now only really working one day a week, which is either a Thursday or a Friday.

When I first began my employment with Druid I was working there as a pretty normal marketing employee. Even when I was at home, I would be on the telephone sorting out one thing or another. I had projects to arrange, with the usual deadlines, and I worked towards them as best I could. Now, by necessity, my input is much more *ad hoc*, and I don't have any continuity in terms of my job function. I can't work on projects that have deadlines because I'm not there for most of the week, and I miss that, because I feel as though I can't get my teeth into anything. As long as I always remember that normal work is just temporarily suspended because of rugby there's no problem, and I can cope with it. But if I were at the beginning of my rugby playing life, with the prospect of another 12 years devoid of mental stimulation, I would be thinking hard about my future in the game. I am not sure that I would just want to think and play rugby and only rugby for 12 years on the trot.

To work or not to work suddenly became a very real issue for all the Bath players when those new club contracts were being signed. You couldn't expect everyone to give up their jobs immediately, because, to be honest, we didn't know how everything would pan out. Professionalism, as we saw it at that stage, might not have worked, so it created an intermediate stage where some people managed to keep their jobs, mainly in cases where the employer took an enormously sympathetic view, with the majority of players moving, albeit gradually, into full-time rugby.

Now most of the younger guys joining in the game at the highest level are moving straight into professional rugby, and have never had 'other jobs'. That may make it easier in time, as everybody in the game will be full time. However, I have no doubt that a total seven-day-a-week rugby focus could create mental problems for players. You only need to look at other professional sports to see the mental anguish which can be caused. Footballers, for instance, would be the first to agree that too much free time was a causal factor in the gambling, drink and drugs problems which seem to assault the careers of some of the most talented players. Rugby will probably have to cope with these new pressures in due course, and it will need to find players other worthwhile things to do around the club and the game. You cannot eat, sleep, train, play and think rugby all week long.

Ben Clarke agrees with me, saying, 'It's important to have a degree of professionalism for your game to improve, but not full-time rugby. I still want an outside interest in the business world.' In time that may no longer be possible, and leading players will probably be forced into an either/or decision. In fact, that day is fast approaching. My own lifestyle is very different, but with a continuing interest in work my mind is still occupied with an occasional mental challenge.

Nowadays, however, I am able to get up after Yolanda four days out of five, whereas when I was 'working' I always needed to be up before her to commute to the office. I would get up at 6.15 a.m. to catch the train to Staines or drive the two-hour journey. Now players need that extra sleep because of the enhanced training. It doesn't matter whether it's from a game or a heavy weights session, you are doing so much physical exercise that you are bound to feel far more tired, and your body needs the rest to recover and repair. That's one reason why playing careers are ultimately bound to be shorter. Not everyone is resting properly. There is an old saying which is very true: 'An athlete rarely over trains, but he invariably under rests.' When players are supposed to be resting and, literally, putting their feet up, many are not. They are out shopping or playing golf. Mentally it may be regarded as a rest, but, in truth, it's not what you really need to be doing physically – although we all do it. You need that quiet rest time because the new training regime really is much more demanding.

In a typical mid-season week, our new training schedule looks something like this. On Mondays and Tuesdays the work-outs are quite physical. We do squad sessions together on both mornings, and then skill work in the afternoons. On Wednesday mornings the training is a little more 'light-hearted'. Sometimes we play basketball or volleyball, but it always tends to be some form of non-contact aerobic exercise. Occasionally, I fit in some extra sprinting on Wednesdays. On Thursday morning we do a sprint session, followed by our final team run-out on Thursday evening. That comprises a variety of defensive work and running through some of our attacking options. Friday is an important rest day before a game. Of course, if we're playing a midweek game the schedule is slightly different.

The changes to our lives have been so dramatic that there were bound to be problems, and it does require a certain amount of physical self-discipline. It's all too easy to kid yourself into believing that you are resting when you're not. And, with the huge amount of free time now on your hands, it would also be too easy to go to the pub for lunch and a couple of beers in the middle of the week. Having said that, I have been surprised, and impressed, at how disciplined the players have generally been in this regard, particularly when it comes to midweek drinking. Bearing in mind the potential for sneaking out and getting wrecked, it hasn't led to any problems – so far! People just haven't done that, which has been great, although we'd notice it if they did, as it would be obvious at training where you can't afford to be anything other than at your best. Of course we still have a few drinks after a game on a Saturday night – after all, that's part and parcel of the game.

In terms of my own drinking I haven't had to change my habits radically. Yolanda and I have always shared a bottle of wine once or twice a week, but we don't drink every night. However, I certainly eat more, and more often. I seem to be continually 'snacking'. Rugby players are traditionally very bad in terms of their dietary approach. Luckily I have a fair amount of dietary training from my days at Cow and Gate, and I know the importance of eating a healthy, balanced diet. We don't follow any special menu at home, but we do try to eat a balance of white and red meat and plenty of vegetables, and I don't eat steak on a Friday.

When I go to an England session, particularly in the build-up to a game, I eat all the time. That's why I used to be terrible when I was on the bench as a replacement. All I ever seemed to do during the build-up week was eat and get fat! Eating and more eating without the hard, focused training that you do when you're in the starting line-up, and no international game at the end of it to burn off the excess energy . . . I often felt completely bloated after I came back from being on the England bench. During a Five Nations campaign I could put on a significant amount of weight over the eight-week period. I have been known to put on 3lbs just like that over the championship; it might not sound a lot, but over eight weeks it is, and in all the wrong places as well. Just ask Yolanda!

CHAPTER FOUR

Style: A Whole New Ball Game

Without doubt the 1995 Rugby World Cup in South Africa was a watershed in terms of the playing style we aspire to in the English game, and the semi-final against New Zealand was the key turning point. To see the All Blacks play that incredibly powerful open running game, where they came at us, again and again, was inspirational, and every man in the squad came home from that experience with new aspirations. These aspirations were almost immediately given added impetus by the announcement that the sport could now be truly 'professional'.

In the run-in to the World Cup, there had been a lot of debate about the forward-dominated English style and its effectiveness, particularly at international level. Many critics felt that England had the measure of the other Five Nations teams playing this very basic forward-oriented game, but had severe doubts about whether we could compete effectively with the sides from the southern hemisphere. With hindsight, those critics had a valid point, although we still managed to scrape past our arch rivals the Wallabies to reach the semi-final. However, the awesome New Zealand performance in that semi-final in Cape Town caused everyone connected with the game here to take another look at how we play rugby. It was the catalyst for dramatic change, and the England players came home to lead the revolution for a more fluid, attractive, running game.

At the beginning of the 1995–96 season, all the Bath players agreed that this was the way they wanted the team to play its rugby in the new 'open' game. We set out wanting to win, but also to entertain. At England level, too, the change was dramatic. The first England meeting we had after the World Cup was fantastic, with everyone in agreement that we should work towards this exciting new open style. Over the five years I have been in the international squad I can honestly say that we have never thought and spoken as one like we did in that meeting. It was amazing, considering that we all came from different clubs and backgrounds, each with a history of playing the game in a different way.

It was a huge sea-change, and just knowing that everyone was committed to playing the game in that way was a major step forward. Yes, it was a somewhat painful learning curve during that international season, and we didn't get everything right on the pitch. But, in many ways, it made it so much easier for Jack and myself last season because everyone in the England set-up was committed to playing the games in that more attacking style. We didn't have to argue out our approach. There was no disagreement.

At the start of the 1995–96 season the club games were so different from those we were used to. They were out of this world in terms of entertainment and enthralling end-to-end rugby. The spectators loved it. But the game had changed so dramatically in such a short time that some of the rugby writers were backtracking and saying 'Let's have a bit of kicking' and 'Let's see some set-piece moves'. It was somewhat ironic, for they were the very people who had been slagging us off for playing ten-man rugby, and suddenly they were hankering for a bit more of it. Those early games were really enjoyable, though.

Without doubt the new style and approach flew home to England with the fired-up World Cup squad, and those players returned to their clubs enthused with a new philosophy and approach. And, having seen the All Blacks demolish our trophy hopes with such style and power, nobody at home could disagree! In the 1996–97 season that spirit of adventure was fuelled by the introduction of a handful of southern hemisphere stars to the Courage League. Men like François Pienaar, Joel Stransky and Michael Lynagh, giants of the international game, came to these shores and generally had a dramatic all-round influence.

Admittedly, that early hunger for running rugby has been tempered by some realism and good sense. The domestic game has pulled back a little bit, and now we do see more tactical kicking and a bit more balance. Jack Rowell is one man who is keen on that balanced approach. He goes on and on about 'a balanced game' in contrast to my approach, which is if the space is on and you have got the ball then you run through it, regardless of where you are on the pitch. When Jack asks me what I would do with the ball on our own line, I say that we should attack, as the All Blacks would. I know my attitude winds him up, and I play on that, not least because he's much more conservative than me in his favoured playing style.

I think it was Ian Jones who said he would attack from anywhere on his own try line, because the defence is much deeper and the opposition are much less switched on. I agree. Dummy scissors, throw the ball wide and run at the opposition! That's the sort of attitude I essentially believe in. But Jack would say, 'Oh no you don't. You kick to touch from there!' Having said that, you do need some of 'Jack's balance', otherwise the opposition will second guess your next move. You always need to be able to surprise the enemy, and there are some times when it will be very much to your advantage to vary the style and work to a much more complex pattern.

In truth, the southern hemisphere teams have an advantage playing that style of all-out attacking rugby, simply because of the way the game is refereed in those countries. Rugby is refereed differently there, and the players do things differently in contact situations. It's very hard to get the ball back in southern hemisphere rugby, unless someone knocks the ball on or you hit the ball out of their hands in the tackle. For instance, when you see some of the Super 10s and Super 12s, it's often a case of one side keeping the ball until they score. The forwards go in, in ones and twos, and it seems as though the ball always comes back.

In contrast, one of the strengths in the British game is nicking the ball on the ground, something the New Zealanders are not used to. In England, you can keep the ball but you have to protect every ruck and maul to stop the opposition from stealing it. It's just a different culture. In Britain it's legal, and we feel very good when we do it. But for some reason they don't allow you to do that in New

Zealand; it's certainly not as prevalent. Because there is more chance of someone nicking the ball from you here, it makes it much harder and more dangerous to attack from your own line. If you are tackled in this position and you haven't got support on hand straightaway, the opposition are probably going to pinch the ball in a perilous situation, so it is often felt to be just too dangerous a strategy. It is quite a big difference, because it means that you don't have so much confidence in all-out attack.

The structure of the southern hemisphere game also has a critical influence on the end result. They have a superb administrative and playing structure in place, and it's something that we need to nurture as quickly as possible. We are moving towards something which is more ideal, with home and away fixtures in Europe in the 1997–98 season, but we're only going to play six games, three at home and three away, as we will play in pools of four. In the southern hemisphere they play more games of that higher standard. In the Super 12s everyone plays everyone else once, home or away, so teams play 11 quality games as a result. The sooner we can increase the number of these even higher quality games, and conversely reduce the number of national league games, the better.

Therein lies the other problem. We have to try and reduce the number of matches in the newly sponsored Allied Dunbar Premiership, because we are asking our top players to play far too many games in the 1997–98 season. A better balance has got to be found and it has got to be found soon. At the moment nothing is giving. There are still 22 league games planned for this season, and some of those will be played midweek. Personally I think it's just too much to ask a professional rugby player to play more than one game a week. In rugby you can't give your best at top pace twice in one week. You may be able to coast through these games, but that's not what we need to be encouraging. The 1997–98 season will start earlier than usual, and it will be a long one. That's not so bad for the clubs with big squads, but it will be hard on the top players in clubs with small squads who will be expected to turn out for every game.

Everyone must realise that this European competition will help sharpen our game. The game Bath played against Cardiff in the

Heineken Cup in the 1996–97 season was as close to an international as anything I have played in at club level, and games like that have got to be the way forward. If we are not able to make this leap in standard, the gap between the playing standards of the northern and the southern hemispheres will continue to increase.

The best way forward would be to have fewer teams in the league, and further development of the European competition to sit alongside the Heineken Cup – in order to improve there needs to be an opportunity for everyone to play in the Euro melting pot. If a club is not playing so many league fixtures, it will need to have meaningful European games in their place. There are also a number of countries who could get involved. Why not include some of the smaller teams in international rugby like Spain, Romania, Germany and Holland in the European club scene? This may help spread the game to a wider European audience. There's nothing to be lost and everything to be gained. This new pan-European competition structure would not be cheap for the clubs. After all, if you are going to play in Bristol it's a lot less expensive than going to Treviso or Bucharest! But I believe that it has to be a step forward.

One day you could even have a northern versus southern hemisphere play-off. That would be a massive occasion. In reality it probably won't happen during my playing career, but you never know. If the sponsorship monies and TV audience are there, anything is possible. With the top two teams in Europe competing against the top two teams in the southern hemisphere, playing a semi-final and a final, it could eventually be one hell of a global competition.

At the moment we still have a long way to go in our game before that can be a competitive reality. The structure of rugby in the southern hemisphere helps breed quality, and we need to take a leaf out of their book. They play the Super 12s, followed by a lot of internationals, so they are playing high-quality games all the time. That's the way we have to go. We are heading in the right direction, but still too slowly. The British game is two years behind physically, in terms of conditioning and fitness, structurally and administratively. But they did turn professional before us, and with that head start have evolved a completely professional attitude. New Zealand rugby, especially, provided players with a good living long before the game went professional anywhere else in the world.

That is one reason why I particularly admire the progressive and highly professional Australian approach to rugby – and it's not even a fanatical rugby nation like New Zealand and South Africa. Rugby is definitely not the number-one game down under, and it has to fight hard with rugby league, Aussie rules football, soccer and cricket for its support. In New Zealand and South Africa rugby is by far and away the dominant participation and viewing sport, so much so that it's almost a religion. It's no wonder the game is so far advanced in these countries. In contrast, football is clearly the number-one sport in Britain, but we haven't managed to cultivate the Aussies' forward-thinking approach to the game of rugby union.

The weather conditions and climate in the southern hemisphere are yet another powerful influence on their dynamic rugby style and structure. However, while it may be cold and wet for much of the year here, that doesn't mean we don't have options which would help us progress in the game and become more competitive on the world stage. You cannot play effective running rugby in the mud and rain, no question, so I think it would help our game if we had a planned winter break. We could comfortably write off 20 December to 20 January each season. In many respects we already do, at least unofficially. Certainly at Bath we are used to postponing a couple of games during this Christmas period, pretty much without exception.

The only way we can carry on in really bad weather is by using hot-air blowers as Bath did in our last home fixture against Saracens, but that's probably not very practical. Otherwise we should have this four-week period as a rest. It would also mean we would be playing on harder, faster pitches later in the season, pitches which are conducive to running, flowing rugby. I really looked forward to playing against Wasps at Loftus Road (more used to staging Queens Park Rangers' football games), because the grass is like a carpet, not unlike many of the pitches used in the Super 12s. If you are playing regularly on those flat, smooth surfaces you are going to be a lot quicker round the pitch, which must be good for you as an athlete. The game will become a lot quicker, and you are gradually going to get used to playing the game at that faster pace. That's why I prefer to play rugby in the spring. I love that time of the season because the grounds are starting to get firm, and it suits my game.

If we had a one-month break over the Christmas period we would lose some continuity, but, as far as I am concerned, that's the only problem. In all other respects it would do the game no end of good. The idea would then be to push the climax of the season right to the end of May. There are some things that only we can decide in the UK, decisions that nobody else is going to make for us, and a one-month winter break is one of them. In most areas of the game, however, we are simply content to sit back and wait for other more progressive nations to take the bull by the horns and move ahead. We talk about style and structure, and what we have learned and can learn from the southern hemisphere game, but why do we always have to be the ones following the rest of the rugby world? Why can't English rugby take some progressive and forward-thinking decisions?

Rule changes are a prime example. Most of the rule changes that are brought into the domestic game have already been introduced and successfully tried and tested in the southern hemisphere. Some years later, we may follow suit. For instance, they have already introduced the ten-minute half-time interval and the rugby league favourite, the 'sin bin'. Why didn't we do these innovative things in the British game first? The southern hemisphere approach always seems to be the more progressive, and I find that really annoying, as well as somewhat baffling. It means that they always seem to be one, two or even three steps ahead, both on and off the pitch. If you can be progressive off the pitch, it certainly helps when it comes to the game on the pitch. It's an approach our administrators and rule-makers must come to understand.

CHAPTER FIVE

Rowell Picks His Man

'DG is always very calm under pressure, and he's a great communicator. Tactically he knows the type of game he wants to play, but he always keeps an open mind on the pitch.'

MIKE CATT

My father had been joking about me becoming the England rugby captain since I was 16 years old, and when Will handed in his captain's armband after the 1996 Five Nations Championship I must admit that I had my eye on the job. It's every schoolboy's dream. However, my first priority has always been to have my name on the England teamsheet, and, after the best part of five years on the bench with only one year playing regularly for England, the captaincy was always a secondary consideration.

There was a long gap between Will's announcement and Jack Rowell's appointment of a new skipper in November 1996, along with plenty of press speculation about the favourites for the role, interwoven with hundreds of column inches about the perilous state of the game and the ongoing row between the RFU and the Courage League One and Two clubs. But when Jack spoke to me about the England captaincy for the first time, I knew then that I was in with a good chance, despite the best guessing of the rugby media. The experts didn't regard me as the first choice, with Lawrence Dallaglio and Jason Leonard in the front row of their stalls coming into the international season. To some of the press corps, I was still a 20–1 outsider. It also didn't help that I was the only injured candidate for the job. In fact, there were a couple of snags standing in Jack Rowell's way if, as has been said, I was always his 'first choice' England captain. One was that knee ligament injury sustained in the game against London Irish in October. And the other was the continued good form of Jerry Guscott and Will Carling, my rivals in the England centre who had kept me on the sidelines for so long.

Jack had said openly that he intended to speak to all of the potential candidates in a sort of job interview before reaching any decision, and I met with him at the Bath Spa Hotel, close to where I live in the city. That initial meeting with Jack was a combination of an interview and a highly focused discussion. As ever, Jack posed some quite provocative questions, and it was obvious he meant business. It wasn't one of those cosy 'How are you getting on, Phil?' chats.

He concentrated on finding out my views on the playing side of things, where the captain can have the most influence: directing the team on the pitch. That was a point in my favour as far as I was concerned. I have always been a firm believer in the captain's job being primarily on the field of play, and not in all of the ancillary nonsense which inevitably comes hand in hand with the role – and this role in particular. It also suited me, because I feel that I am a good strong leader with a sharp tactical rugby mind. With a League and Cup double behind me in my first season in charge of Bath, I also had some valuable experience to bring to the party. And I'd managed to cut a swathe through the maze of politics at Bath during that double-winning season, something else which must have helped my rugby CV.

Jack was interested in what I would do with the England team, and how I'd want to do it. He asked me how England should play, and what changes I would make, if any. He also quizzed me about my approach to the captaincy, and what my current England dream XV would be. What Jack didn't do at the interview was ask me how I would deal with the press, nor ask about the added media pressures, although I think that these questions must have also been in his mind when he made the final decision.

Jack played it cool and gave nothing away. I expected no more. He certainly didn't give me any indication that I was going to be the next skipper, but that's the way he always tends to operate. You always have to be very careful about jumping to conclusions after meeting with him, because you can never know what he's thinking. He hides his thoughts and emotions so well. He's a shrewd businessman with a reputation for keeping his men 'on edge', something he does very effectively, so I didn't want to get too excited after the meeting, although I felt it had gone very well. Part of me came home thinking that I could be the next England captain; the emotional side of my character certainly thought it could be me. But the more rational side was screaming, 'No, don't even think about it, because you could so easily be disappointed!'

Following that preliminary discussion in Bath, a whole month went by and very little happened until just before the announcement was made on 5 November. Jack had rung me up a couple of times on Sunday nights, asking for my opinion about who should play at fly-half and about my thoughts on some of the other players who should be selected for the first international of the season. The number ten shirt was under the media spotlight, and Jack wanted to talk through the options. But even then I didn't get carried away, because I know what he is like. It could have been everything and nothing. In fact, my first reaction was 'sod you'. I thought it was a bit of a cheek, asking me about the pros and cons of other players without mentioning anything about me playing in the England team, or the captaincy. I was damned if I was going to mention it either! I wasn't going to let him think that I was sitting around waiting on his every word. Knowing the man as I do, I was sure he was playing some of the same mind games with Lawrence and Jason. However, when I'd mentioned the skipper's job to them in a quiet moment, I got the distinct impression that Jack had spoken to me in confidence a lot more often. Once again it inevitably set me thinking that I could be in with a real chance.

The weekend before the announcement was finally made, I was fit and travelled to play in Bath's big European Cup game away against Treviso. We understood that there was going to be a press conference about the England captaincy on the Tuesday, so I assumed Jack was bound to tell the new captain, whoever he was, sometime during the weekend, probably on the Sunday. When I arrived home from the Treviso game that Sunday there was no message on the answerphone, and I naturally assumed that I hadn't got the job. I wasn't desperately disappointed, and I forced it to the back of my mind, trying not to dwell on what I thought was now the missed opportunity. It was quiet – all too quiet – on that Sunday night. Nobody phoned at all. It was only on the Monday that things started to happen, 24 hours before the press conference and some eight months after Will's retirement as captain! Talk about last minute.

I was working at home on the Monday morning with plans to play golf in the afternoon. After the long trip to Treviso, John Hall had given us the Monday afternoon off so Henry Paul, Jon Callard (JC), Jon Sleightholme (Sleights) and I planned a round at Orchardleigh Golf Club on the outskirts of Frome, Somerset. I was literally walking out of the door when Jack telephoned me and, without any explanation, asked me to phone him back at 2.30 p.m. 'sharp'. End of conversation. It was only then that the butterflies really started. It was about 12.30 p.m. as I stepped out of the door, so I had two nervous hours to sweat on what was happening – or not happening.

I said nothing to the boys. There was the usual caustic banter between the four of us that afternoon. I took the (RFU-sponsored!) mobile phone with me, against all course regulations, but I didn't mention anything about having to call Jack. I still wasn't sure. We started to play the round, and at the start of the third hole I made a few excuses and sidled off to make my call. 2.30 p.m. precisely. But Jack's line was engaged, and I remember thinking, 'Damn it.' I drove to the edge of the green on the par-three third hole and that was a good opportunity to try him again, and this time I managed to get through. His first words were typically abrupt. 'You're late,' he said. But then he added, 'You'll nevertheless be pleased to know that we have selected you as the captain of England.'

I was taken aback. I really hadn't expected him to give me the job, despite thinking that I was the right man! Jack swore me to secrecy because the press conference was still a day away, but he did say that I could tell Yolanda and my parents if they promised to keep it quiet. Then he spent ten minutes talking about international team selection for the first game against Italy, while my golfing partners watched in amazement. The guys must have realised it was important, because they let me carry on with the call undisturbed, although I did get some serious gip about having my mobile phone on the golf course when I eventually finished the conversation.

I went back to the golf and, for once, I played five magnificent holes. I chipped on to the green and holed the putt to halve the third, and went on to play better than I have ever played, and probably better than I will ever play again. Let it be said that nothing puts a de Glanville off his stroke! I was on a high, and the adrenalin was rushing.

I called Yolanda, who is a maths teacher and 'Miss Keverne' to her class. She must have known immediately that the job was mine because I'd said I would only drag her away from a class if I had any good news to report. She received a note midway through a lesson asking her to phone me urgently, so she knew. When Yolanda called me back she had to be incredibly 'matter of fact' because she was phoning from the secretary's office, and couldn't give the game away. 'Uh, uh, that's good to know,' she said casually. 'Well done.' Later she told me that she wanted to scream 'Yeeeeeees!'. Returning to her class, Yolanda brought the lesson to a close and let the kids out early. They knew that something was going on, because she has a reputation for never letting them out before the bell, but the kids were way off track with their guesses. *They thought that she was pregnant!*

I also phoned my parents, and spoke to dad. 'Dad,' I said, 'I can't believe it. It's me!' They were chuffed to bits. Dad told me that it was the 'fulfilment of their dreams'. He says that I've always had the ability to step back from the battle and say, 'This isn't going the right way,' and then make the necessary changes on the field to make things work better. I was going to need that ability more than ever now.

That night Yolanda and I went round to my sister's house in Bath and the three of us celebrated with a bottle of champagne. We began to speculate about what might come next. The announcement was made on Guy Fawkes Day, 5 November, and whatever I had done I could not have prepared myself for the fireworks which followed amidst the huge media interest. It was one hell of a demanding day and very exhausting. Complete mayhem.

The press conference was a glitzy business, a fanfare of trumpets and a blaze of flashlights greeting my arrival on the stage. The 'event' was even broadcast on Radio 5 Live. Jack said, 'We've had eight months to think about it and there have been several outstanding candidates. Now is the time for someone new to put his stamp on the side, to thrust it to the forefront of the world game and to bring a positive attitude to the way we play at international level. It is a big challenge for Phil and yet the new captain has already had success at Bath with that weight of expectation on his shoulders.' It was proof positive that my track record at Bath had swayed the vote my way. Jack added some other kind words, saying, 'Phil can lead us where we want to go, win today, win tomorrow, and on to the World Cup. He is able to make the necessary decisions under fire, and can change things when needed.'

The press conference was just a taster of the media circus which ensued afterwards. It seemed like everyone wanted five minutes of my time. That's where my agent, Ashley Woolfe of the James Grant Group, really helped out. They look after some big stars like Anthea Turner and Philip Schofield as well as some of my friends in the rugby world like Lawrence Dallaglio, Andy Gomarsall and Alex King, and they are well used to taking some of the day-to-day strain off the people they look after. They took as much of the pressure off me as they could right from the start, filtering the interviews and appearances, but even with their help that first week was just crazy. People I'd never even heard of were telephoning my mobile and home numbers, and in the end we had to put the answering service on the mobile and unplug the BT line at home.

There was, of course, an immediate debate about the merits of my appointment, and about whether the captain should be picked game by game, or for the season. Jack Rowell believed in me, and now I had to convince the public. I was glad that I was picked as the

England captain for the entire season, and not just because it was me, but because it's what the job demands. The influence of the captain is significant in terms of the overall culture of the team, the feeling within the squad, and its development. A winning team is also a settled team. There needs to be continuity, not change, and a regular captain helps. Any player's form will fluctuate game to game across a season, and if the skipper is playing badly then yes, he may be dropped. But the captain's contribution to the overall well-being of the side should not be undervalued, and making the appointment for a season – but no more than a season – must be the right approach for the future.

I felt the captain's role would be a challenge, and told the press as much, but I have always been a fierce competitor and nothing fazes me. I certainly wasn't daunted by the prospect of wearing the captain's badge. And though I knew the appointment would change my life forever, I set out to keep my feet firmly on the ground. Yolanda said she would see to that! We sat down on the night I heard about the new job and decided that we were going to make a conscious effort to ensure it would not change our lives too much. I want to make sure that it doesn't, because I firmly believe that the captain is ultimately just another player, and should be nothing more, in the eyes of either the media or his teammates.

Will Carling congratulated me both in print and in private. He said that he thought I had been an 'excellent captain' for Bath and would be for England. He was a hard act to follow because he had done such fantastic things for English rugby, in effect launching the country to the forefront of world rugby, which was something his predecessors were unable to achieve. But it was time for a change. It needed someone new to come in and take things forward. I had been in the squad for nearly five years, I knew the players, and I knew how things were run. I felt I could do the job with some aplomb. It also helped that I had already earned the respect of my teammates. Jerry Guscott and Catty both told reporters that they were delighted, and confirmed that I had 'earned' that respect from my fellow players during the time I had been knocking on the international door.

There were a lot of distractions off the field during 1996, and in the last two or three months before that announcement it got worse than ever. For me the main challenge was therefore to refocus everybody on to what was happening on the field of play, and to pull everything together so that, from the very start, the team could get their heads round playing against a very difficult Italian side.

I am a leader on the field, and want to take control. I love running the game where I can, and while I told the press that I wanted England to play an open and attractive game, I tempered that with a little realism. You need to have a balanced game to keep the opposition guessing. First and foremost we set out to enjoy ourselves, and the best way to do that is to win with the whole team contributing to the game. We needed to strike the right balance within the squad. You can't just throw the ball wide for the sake of doing it. It simply becomes too predictable. There are times too when you need to tie the game down, to play the touchlines, to probe the blindside, maybe to exploit a weakness or to tie in the defence which is lining up. These are just a few of the possibilities. You've got to be able to read it on the run. You need to be instinctive, to be able to sum up in an instant the most suitable alternative. What I wanted us to aim at was to be more varied in our attack and to bring the forwards and backs together as often as possible. I wanted us to be more effective and to win games by working to a more complex pattern. It so happened that I felt that this style was, and still is, probably easier on the eye and more entertaining. But, make no mistake, it's a means to an end, not an end in itself. The more integrated approach is the way to win matches in the modern era. Personally, I may not be as thrusting as Will or as smooth and elegant as Jerry, but I can do those right things at the right times, and I believe there are few better decision-makers under pressure.

I quickly found that captaincy brought with it a number of added responsibilities, although I don't expect that most of my England teammates are aware of a lot of them – William David Charles Carling OBE excepted, of course! Quite a few of the new responsibilities are media-related, and I am convinced that the next

England captain should have at least some basic media training. I sat next to English Cricket Board boss Sir Ian MacLaurin at a dinner not so long ago, and he said that England cricket skipper Mike Atherton wasn't given any media training either. That training ought to be a priority, especially as the captain of any England team is continually in the media spotlight.

It is also important for the team that the captain is always conveying the right message and mood in front of the press. What you say at that press conference on a Wednesday is widely quoted in Thursday's and Friday's newspapers and TV reports. If they read and hear those reports and you're saying the wrong things, it does nothing for team spirit and morale. The players will invariably extract the most negative vibes, and that's the last thing you want in the build-up to a game.

You need everything to be as settled as possible for the team in that build-up week and if at any stage you are saying things that are controversial, it can act to the contrary. I am particularly aware of this responsibility, and I don't want to do anything which could 'upset the apple-cart'. If things have got to be said I will say them, but in private, because one of my main tasks is to make sure that the team is in the right frame of mind to play and win on the Saturday. While I am skipper I want the team to be as well prepared as it possibly can be, and crystal clear about how we are going to play the next game. They don't need a confusing message coming from me via the sports pages.

My off-the-field role took up a lot of time at the beginning of the season, as we had a number of new England caps coming in for their first games. I was especially keen to try and get the balance of the team's week just right, and early on I tinkered with the mix in terms of making sure there was enough relaxation and enough hard work in the build-up. For instance, we may have planned a meeting for 6 p.m. on a Thursday evening before an international. But if, on the Thursday morning, I sensed it was going to be too much for the lads, I said so to Jack, and we cancelled or rearranged.

As part of my new role I have an input into team selection, although Jack ultimately makes the final decisions. With so many talented players in the wings, some of those selection decisions are marginal; there is so little to choose between players, and that makes it very difficult. Other decisions are easier. At the moment, for example, Martin Johnson will always be the first name on the team-sheet.

Although I have a job to do off the field, I think I have plenty to offer on it as well, particularly in terms of decision-making and tactics across 80 minutes. As the captain, I'm now calling many of the moves during the game, which sets my style of captaincy apart from that of Will. He was more happy to leave decision-making up to his seasoned generals, men like Rob Andrew.

I think that the single most important factor which led to Jack choosing me ahead of Lawrence and Jason is my tactical awareness, resulting from experience gleaned from my baptism of fire as Bath skipper in 1995–96, and my rugby background. I think that it would now be very hard for somebody to become the England captain without having captained his club. I believe that tactical experience is crucial, despite the fact that some people say it's easier these days now that the coach can come on at half-time and sort things out. That may be so, but what happens when things are going wrong and the coach is not around? While I am captain I'll be leading from the front, and on the pitch I make the decisions. It's an area in which I believe I am relatively strong.

Will never did take on that tactical role, leaving it instead to Deano and to Rob. It must have hacked him off that I was calling some of the moves last season. But that's what I wanted to do, and I needed the control over those options. Nevertheless, Will was marvellous in terms of the way he settled back into being a player without the captaincy on his shoulders. He clearly began to enjoy his rugby again. He seemed to settle into a more relaxed lifestyle, and a new (lower) public profile helped improve his relationship with the other lads. Last season he sat at the meal table with the other players instead of being on the top table, and it's little things like that that make a big difference. And on the field he was superb. Will was also supportive to me, and in the early stages of my new job as captain he would ask me how it was going. We wouldn't discuss it at any length, but on occasions he would offer snippets of his experiences.

There are a few so-called 'perks' which come with the captaincy, such as having your own hotel bedroom in the days before an international, but I'm not one for all that. The other players all share a room, so that is what I am used to. Funnily enough, I am not that happy about having my own room and would rather be sharing with a teammate and enjoying that pre-match banter, but the problem is, who would I share with? There are some things which need to be said in private, and you can't get the privacy you need with a roomy. However, I certainly don't think that I ought to get any special treatment just because I am the England captain.

I don't want to jazz the role up too much or talk about its high-profile nature. I come back to Will because I think he fell into that trap, partly because his own day-to-day business evolved around that high profile, and partly because he got caught up in things off the field which drew him into a different world of celebrity status. It has been my intention to step back from the hype and the fantasy world wherever possible, and to keep the role of captain in perspective. I want people to see the job for what it is, so I made a conscious effort not to go singing and dancing about what it entails because I thought that it would be bad for the team. I think my approach may have been one of the secondary reasons why Jack appointed me to succeed Will. I have a very clean direct relationship with Jack, which helps. I am quite prepared to turn round to him and say 'no' in certain situations – or to anybody else for that matter.

However, I too have now been thrust into the spotlight, albeit one which is less intense than that which Will was under, and now it's me having to be careful about what I say and do. The England captaincy brings with it pressures that you can't understand until the job is yours, but I wanted to make sure that the inevitable press comment and speculation was now focused entirely on rugby and the game we play, rather than anything that I do off the pitch. I think I have succeeded. It does the players no good to have a captain who has such a high profile that he is on a different level and they can't talk to him, they can't relate to him, and they can't take the mickey out of him. You have got to be able to give and take stick with your teammates. There's nothing scientific about that approach to man management on or off the sportsfield!

What I brought to the Bath team in terms of my approach to captaincy, I try to bring to the England set-up. I try to stay as relaxed as I can for as much of the time as possible, and then switch on and focus when it is required, during the training sessions and the team meetings. By the time it gets to the Friday before a major game I start winding myself up psychologically and physically. And that's what I want from my players.

In many ways it's easier to captain Bath, because I have more contact with the players and that allows me to get to know them better. When you are the England captain you go for long periods without seeing or even speaking to your fellow players. It makes it more difficult to bond and to develop that close understanding that comes from time spent together; you can't judge their moods, learn how they function, and know how each individual responds to different situations. You can do that at Bath, where we virtually eat, sleep and drink together now that we're professional.

It's also easier in terms of the training and the technical aspects of the game. When we train at Bath everybody knows what they are doing without the need for a discussion. When we train with the England team, however, there are always a number of options, because every player brings ideas and a playing style from his own club, and we need to discuss, take playing decisions and define a clear strategy. It is a key difference; not everybody is sure about the next move in certain international situations, whereas at Bath you instinctively know what happens next.

As the first international game of the 1996–97 season against Italy approached, Jack and I spoke at length about whether to play me alongside Jerry Guscott, my usual club partner at centre for Bath. Centre was just one of the many positions debated by the press during the season. In 1994 I had played a season at centre with Will, and I had felt then that we weren't really very effective. So I argued that the pairing should be either Guscott and Carling or

Guscott and de Glanville – but not Carling and de Glanville.

Prior to the Italy match I felt it should be Guscott and de Glanville. I never thought for one moment that I should have been on the bench. I reckoned I had finally earned my big chance after more than 20 games on the touchline and was now hungry to prove myself in the international arena. In the end, Will partnered me in that game and for the rest of the international season. He played extremely well, and we worked well together. Having been pensioned-off the international scene by the press before the season started, Will made a glorious case for the over-30s. Indeed, Mr Carling fully deserved his place after those stirring early performances.

My argument for playing Jerry was nothing to do with personalities, and it was nothing whatsoever to do with Will having been my predecessor as skipper. It was purely about getting the balance of the team right, and I felt that Jerry was the better option. Jack took the decision to play Will, though, and on reflection it was a good one, although Jerry came on a few times and looked at the top of his game.

Jerry is one of the most gifted footballers in the country, perhaps in the world. When he's good, he's the best. But when he's bad, and it has been known, he's horrid. When he is not playing on song he has the habit of turning too early with his back to the oncoming forwards instead of trying to make that extra half-yard; inevitably he will then get thumped and driven backwards. That means it's very difficult for our forwards to support him. It's one of the faults in his game. It just shows he's not perfect, but then nobody is. Perhaps more importantly, Jack still has a question mark over Jerry's willingness for the battle, for getting his hands dirty and getting stuck in. It's not a matter of Jerry lacking any physical strength or not being able to put in a tackle; far from it, he is one of the strongest players around. In Jack's mind I reckon it's more about whether Jerry is really prepared to 'mix it', and I think that was probably one of the primary reasons why he wasn't selected as first choice in the 1996–97 season, along with Will's good form. Jerry comes on and shows flashes of brilliance – and he is brilliant

– but it's all about being able to do that consistently for 80 minutes and playing your part in the wider game.

I didn't get to lead the team out against Italy in my first international as skipper. It was Jason Leonard's 50th cap and he ran out first with me behind. It was still a magic moment, although by that stage I was so focused on the game that it almost passed unnoticed. Unless you have actually played rugby – or another big team sport – at that level, you cannot imagine the extraordinary feeling when you run out on to the pitch before an international. If you are in the right frame of mind, you hear the anthems and then it's 'total focus'; you could be in another world for the next 80 minutes. You don't hear the crowd at all during the game.

That's how I felt when I ran on to the pitch against Italy. I was more focused than ever before because of the added responsibility and pressure. I loved it! All I was doing was concentrating 100 per cent on how we were going to play the game and what we were going to do in certain situations, because you only ever get a split second to think about the call. There's a lineout, or a scrum, and a decision needs to be made instantly. Suddenly everybody is looking at the skipper! You need to be one step ahead, thinking about what could happen before it does. And when it does, you need to be mentally alert so that you make the right decision.

We introduced five new caps into the starting line-up for the Italy game along with two on the replacements' bench, including 16-stone Chris Sheasby, Tim Stimpson and Andy Gomarsall. I had a quiet word with the new caps who were starting the game on the Thursday beforehand, but after that there was no need for any gimmicks to get them motivated. There was little opportunity for them to find their feet. There is no honeymoon period in international rugby. It is always a special moment when you make your debut, but we needed the new players to contribute from the very first whistle.

We were also aware that we couldn't be complacent. The highly experienced Italian side came to play us at Twickenham having pushed the Wallabies and Scotland very close, and beaten Ireland. They came to prove that they should be part of the Five Nations

Championship, and to make it as difficult for us as possible. With more than 50 caps between their half-backs Troncon and Dominguez, and with the skills of Vaccari, they sent a clear warning signal to our inexperienced debutants.

But we rattled up more than 50 points in a terrific 54–21 victory, and all but wiped out the men in blue. Simon Shaw's jumping in the lineout was telling but his work rate around the field was what really impressed me, and Catty put their midfield under constant pressure. His place-kicking was also a plus, despite an early nerve-racking miss in front of the posts. Chris Sheasby was excellent, fast and powerful, and Andy Gomarsall scored two tries in a sensational first appearance. Ade Adebayo also made a sparkling debut and made one superb break which should have led to a try. In fact, all of the new caps did well, and that was probably the most pleasing aspect of the whole afternoon. I would have liked to have got Tim Stimpson into the action a little more, but his time will come.

If we had kept our minds on the job throughout the game we would not have let in the Italians for three tries in a ten-minute spell in the second half, and we might have won by even more. Having been 35 points up, we let them get back into the game before scoring two late tries ourselves to break the 50-mark. It was a very encouraging start to my England captaincy. There were things we needed to work on, however. We needed to tidy up our defence, which lost its concentration and organisation, something we knew we had to get right before taking on the New Zealand Barbarians the following week. And we needed to think about getting our wide game moving more frequently. But all in all it was highly satisfactory.

And yet, despite the victory, I felt annoyed with the reaction of some of the rugby writers. We scored 54 points against a good side in the first game of the new international season and my first game as skipper, but some of the press still managed to damn us with faint praise. After Italy's string of good results against top opposition, I could not believe it. Why are they so underrated, when they have strength and experience in such depth? If anyone had said to me beforehand that we were going to win and score over 50 points I would have thought they were joking. We would have considered

25–10 a good win against Italy, particularly as we played with seven new caps. I felt that some of those rugby journalists – who should know better – came after us. In hindsight, had they known about the Italian victory over France after the Five Nations in March, perhaps we would have received the credit we deserved. All of the players knew that it was a good result, and when the Italians later rolled over the French we could not help being more than a little smug. Anybody who believes that Italy haven't arrived is sorely mistaken.

If the Italian team had won their game against France in the spring as part of a new enhanced Six Nations tournament, England would have topped last season's championship table. There is no doubt that the Italians are now good enough to play their part, and many of my fellow players feel, as I do, that they should be included in the championship. It must happen. If we want a strong northern hemisphere game we need as many good-quality games as possible, and nowadays the Italians provide extremely stiff opposition. The French agree. In the programme for the France versus Italy game, French Federation president Bernard Lapasset argued for the inclusion of the Italians in a new go-faster championship, even before his side's 40–32 defeat. It was Italian rugby's finest moment, and it put their case forward in the strongest possible fashion. What more do they have to do?

On the evening of the final Five Nations game against Wales I sat next to Welsh Rugby Union chairman Vernon Pugh at the special dinner, and we discussed why the Italians are still excluded from the forthcoming championship plans. 'It's purely a question of money,' he told me. Apparently 'it costs' to put on an international in Italy. But I can't believe that a Six Nations involving the Italians wouldn't more than cover the additional costs. Surely their participation would add extra interest, and more income would be generated instantly?

That media experience after the England victory over Italy brought me back down to earth and actually taught me to ignore what people write and say because, in the final analysis, it doesn't make any difference. I now realise and accept, albeit grudgingly, that it's never going to be perfect.

It was good to move quickly from that game into another home fixture against the New Zealand Barbarians, because we were pitted against one of the very best teams around and we had a genuine opportunity to measure our progress. And, on the day, I don't think that we were far off the pace, although the *Daily Mirror's* headline in the days leading up to the game, 'I'm Jonah get you!', may have been a little over the top. Sean Fitzpatrick said that it was a bit of fun, but that was bullshit. They were certainly 'full on' for that game and they had been 'full on' for it since the summer. They came over to avenge their defeat at Twickenham in 1993, and even though they were missing their world-class centres you would only need to ask the guys who were playing in their place if they were any less committed. No way! It may not have been classified as a Test, but it was a huge test for us.

Fitzpatrick told journalist Mick Cleary that he had come to terms with the Rugby World Cup final defeat by South Africa by being 'philosophical'. 'After all,' he commented, 'it's only a game.' Cleary didn't believe him for one minute, and neither did I. That's not the Fitzpatrick I know. Everyone knows that rugby in New Zealand is much more than that, especially when you don that famous black shirt. So we expected a hard, probing match against these young, exciting NZ Barbarians, particularly as they had ten All Blacks making up the heart of the side, with the huge presence of Fitzpatrick leading the charge.

The Kiwis beat us 34–19, and I thought that although we were caught out on a number of occasions, some of our approach play was as good as anything I had seen from an England team for years. The build-up to our two tries, from Sleights and Tim Stimpson – tries which took us into a 19–13 lead – were both excellent. First Andy Gomarsall's wide pass put Sleights in, and then Will Carling's half break helped put Tim over. The driving play of our forwards in the loose and the delivery of the ball in the tackle was superb, and our backs and forwards interlinked very well. Yes, once or twice we ran out of options, handling was sometimes iffy, passes went astray, and the punting was scrappy – all problems of a technical nature that we can put right. I got caught when I was looking for someone to pass to and everyone was buried at the bottom of the ruck. Those are the sort of situations we have to work on in the future, the fourth and fifth phases, when people are on the floor. The build-up to that point was good. The question is, what do we do then?

Tim Stimpson had a big game. There was one tackle he put in on the NZ centre, as he was poised to score, which justified his place in one. Shaw, Sheasby and Dallaglio also played well. There was a great deal of passion and commitment, but across the 80 minutes they were, on balance, perhaps quicker, stronger and a tad more skilful. The Barbarians nevertheless showed us the task ahead, and it was a valuable exercise. I wasn't too pessimistic about the defeat, and I felt that we were fundamentally sound, especially in the set pieces. At one stage we even looked as though we could win the game. We were 19–13 up and should have turned the screw when we led, but we didn't. We just lost it there. Instead the Kiwis realised they could lose, and it was almost as if they stepped up a gear or two. They never know when to lie down.

It was different in the pre-Christmas game against the Pumas. I admit we had a poor day against Argentina, although we played some good rugby in the last ten minutes. Those ten-minute spells can make or break you. Leaving aside the technical approach, we just weren't up for it enough. I don't think we thought that they were enough of a challenge, and we were wrong. Perhaps we didn't feel as though we had to try very hard to beat them, and that showed. We didn't have the same hunger to win as we had had in the previous games. We didn't have the urgency and passion you need for any international. It was the sort of game I have played in at club level, where players take the field and try to do just enough. You just can't take that sort of approach into an international game these days, though, and it was very disappointing for all concerned.

I had picked up a thigh strain and couldn't play, and it was hard watching the match from the stands. In fact, as new-boy captain I was gutted I couldn't take my place on the field, especially as I'd played so well against Harlequins just a few days before. I sat watching Jason Leonard don the captain's armband and the old centre pairing of Carling and Guscott take over, but, despite their quality and experience, everything we had done in the build-up went up in smoke.

However, the important thing about the Argentina game was that we still came away as winners, even though we didn't play to our potential. Cold comfort for the fans, admittedly, but still an important point. The gaps between teams are closing at international level as well as at top club level. You only need to look at the results against Italy and Argentina. There are rarely 70-pointers at this level any more. A victory is a victory, whoever it's against and however it's achieved. It's the sign of a good team if you can play badly and still win – ask Manchester United! If we can win by playing well and playing open, attractive, running rugby, that's great. But when push comes to shove, I'll take the win however it comes.

The trouble is that the rugby press just loves to pounce on the English team after a game, win or lose, and we don't get the applause we deserve for the many good things we do, or have tried to do – just lambasted for the bad moments. It's not just the England rugby team either, it's any top English sporting stars. Why do we do it? No other nation takes such delight in knocking its sportsmen down a peg or three.

It's also difficult because, more often than not, the rugby writers are able to have their say before we get a chance to talk things through and iron out problems behind the closed doors of the dressing-room. At present the squad doesn't get the chance to meet up to discuss the game immediately afterwards, and on occasions the hacks have piled in and created issues where there weren't any, and problems where none existed before. It just makes the job that much harder. For example, there was an ongoing debate throughout the 1996–97 season about who should be playing first at centre, then at fly-half, and then in the back row. On the whole it was a daily diet of criticism for the players in the team. Everything was dissected under the media spotlight again and again, and it put players under unnecessary pressure when what they really needed was nothing more than a bit of support and encouragement.

I told the players concerned not to get too worried about the speculation, and to carry on as normal wherever possible. I said that there will occasionally be team changes, but that you just can't let the media criticism get to you. 'Don't worry about what they're thinking,' I said. 'Jack's the man you need to convince.' But it is unsettling, and it never ceases to amaze me how we as a nation love sniping at our sporting stars. I know that it comes with the job, and that the reporters have got to 'dig the dirt' and try and create a story. I also know that they need to be controversial, even if they don't believe what they are writing is true. Now I've seen it close up, I realise that you have to have thick skin and be able to sit back and let them have their say. On the pitch you've got to ignore the war of words and do the best you can. There was a hell of a lot of good rugby played last season. That's why I thought, 'Forget it – whatever we do is not going to be good enough' when I saw some of those early press reports.

Can you imagine what it would have been like if we had beaten the New Zealand Barbarians? It would have been absolutely lethal for us to win against a team of that calibre after a couple of games. The public and the press would have been trumpeting England as future world-beaters when we are not yet good enough. That defeat was good for us. It was a stiff lesson because we had a hard game, and we came close to victory – but not nearly close enough. The New Zealanders are still a long way ahead of us. They got it right from the beginning and it will take us a couple of years to catch up. But now I think we really do have the southern hemisphere teams in our sights, and we're chasing harder than ever.

CHAPTER SIX

Jack Rowell: A Man of Mystery

It takes tough men to take tough decisions, and England manager Jack Rowell is one of the breed. But Jack often moves in mysterious and unpredictable ways, and he is no less of a mystery to me now than he was way back in 1990 when I first joined him at Bath. He hasn't forgotten our first meeting! I didn't know Jack Rowell from Adam, so when he introduced himself I said, 'Who are you?'

Jack's own rugby career was interrupted by a neck injury, but what he failed to achieve on the pitch he has most certainly achieved in his role as coach. With Bath RFC he became one of the most successful coaches ever in British sport, winning the John Player/ Pilkington Cup eight times and the Courage League on five occasions. He has also been a highly successful businessman, so his huge managerial talents are indisputable.

Jack became England coach in April 1994, and it's generally assumed that since then he has been trying to wean the side away from set-piece rugby to play a looser, more flexible style.

He has overseen that development, and encouraged his players to strike out in this new direction. But most of this change in emphasis and direction emanated not from Jack, but from the players themselves. In fact, in playing terms Jack is far more conservative in his style and approach. He is the voice of reason and common sense on the pitch rather more than the cavalier free spirit.

What he does supremely well is gather his players around him and get them to take the tactical and playing decisions 'as one' – which invariably take into account his own observations and suggestions. Then he motivates the team to put their common playing strategy into practice on the pitch, an approach which is much easier than a bully-boy coach forcing his own will on a group of headstrong rugby players.

Jack plays an important role in the pre-match sessions simply by the way he operates. He encourages players to come forward and say how they want to play the game, often picking on one man to lead the meeting while he stands in the background. But he is always close by, watching and listening, bringing pragmatism and detail to the overall scheme of things, and acting as a counterbalance to some of the more fanciful things we talk about in tactical terms. Jack brings realism to our game. I might provoke him by suggesting that we should do something innovative and attack-minded from our own line, something daft and dangerous, and Jack will snap back, 'No you won't, you'll kick it to touch!' He also doesn't miss much. Jack will always pick up on things that we have missed, and make sure that we've got everything covered. He's got a great eye for detail.

The *Guardian*'s rugby correspondent Robert Armstrong once said, 'Rowell has always regarded coaching as a process of fine tuning players and creating a mature environment in which they can take on greater responsibility for strategy the closer the match gets.' That gets right to the heart of his ability, and not every coach has that talent, together with the ability to put it into practice effectively with a ramshackle group of feisty 16-stone rugby internationals!

Jack is a shrewd and sharp operator, and there can be no doubt that it is success and the pursuit of success that makes him tick, in sport as well as in business. But he is an enigma, and can be somewhat strange and off-beat in the way he works. I hunted out a cutting of mine from David Miller in *The Times*, written in June 1995, which illustrates this sly and cunning nature. 'If [Geoff] Cooke was the clerical strategist, Rowell is the platoon commander: but always, as Carling observed, intriguingly, from "behind a tree"! . . . Rowell has introduced subtleties which keep everyone on edge.'

Jack is continually trying to give the players around him a kick up the backside, and he loves nothing more than to wind them up and set them off against each other. He is an uncomfortable character, and likes to make others around him uncomfortable too in order to maintain an edge and to keep the players sharp and keen. He can spot a weakness at 100 paces, and hit it from 50. Time and time again he will throw rivals into the ring to slug it out in training, but rarely, if ever, do these mind games move on to the public stage. He keeps it all within the camp.

Even before the first 1997 Five Nations game against Scotland, he called me on the phone and had me at it. Jack asked me whether I felt I should be playing in the team. That was typical Rowell, winding up the new skipper so that he is on the top of his form. 'De Glanville needs a good game,' he said, and then he asked what I would 'bring to the team'. Being well used to this blunt and unfeeling approach, I took no notice whatsoever! Since his days at Bath he hasn't changed much in terms of the way he winds people up. He still manages to find someone's Achilles' heel and kick it.

He also enjoys disrupting training with new ideas and strategies, even at key sessions. At Bath he used to throw something new into the frame only a couple of days before a big game, something completely different and alien to the training that had gone before, and he still does that with England. He'll ask people to do something different on a Thursday before an international, and that's the last thing you want or need in terms of good preparation. The ideal is to be settled and confident about what you are doing, and, in this respect, Jack can be a loose cannon.

He'll often follow his instinct, using gut feeling to get a hook on the character of a player as well as playing ability. This use of the heart instead of the head doesn't always work. I think we saw an example of that when he added the retired England fly-half legend Rob Andrew to the England squad for the match against Wales during the 1996–97 season, when Paul Grayson was injured and Mike Catt moved back into the team at number ten. Young stand-off Alex King, who was already in the training squad, was very upset, and I couldn't blame him. I believe Jack was using the squad system to give all the lads some experience of the build-up and preparations. He didn't necessarily want to be forced into using it as a pecking order, so players outside the starting XV could automatically be the next in line for selection if there were injuries. That's fine, but he should have made that quite clear to everyone at the start. Thereby lies one of his main failings – communication.

Jack can also be a poor man manager. He is a chicken when it comes to telling people that they are going to be or have been dropped, and why they have been dropped. He just doesn't like it, and while I admit that it's the hardest part of the job – because you know how important selection is to everyone concerned – wherever possible he seems to shy away from such man management responsibilities. He is also not very good when it comes to thinking about other people's feelings – and even big lumbering rugby players have feelings. Jack will do what he thinks is right and cut right to the heart of the matter without messing, and there will be no mollycoddling or sympathy afterwards. It means that sometimes he can be very abrupt, and afterwards someone has to pick up the emotional wreckage.

As far as the current crop of players is concerned, I would not therefore describe Jack as a 'popular' coach, but he certainly has their respect, and that's probably the best mix to have in his position. A coach, or the person who is making the selection decisions, shouldn't necessarily be popular, because otherwise he may not be able to make those tough calls that are often necessary. I know that some of the players are unhappy with his management style and approach, and some don't even like him as a person, but Jack never asked to be liked. He has got one or two favourites among the players such as Ben Clarke, whom he gets on really well with, but that doesn't mean he picks him – far from it. My old Bath teammate Stuart Barnes was also a big favourite, but Jack picked Rob Andrew ahead of Stuart. That's life!

Off the pitch Jack is just as much of an enigma, and as hard to read today as he always has been. I suppose that's one of his most valuable weapons, and one of the keys to his success. Those talents have certainly helped him become a successful businessman, and he brings that businesslike manner to work in the world of rugby.

As I write, there has been speculation that Jack is considering giving up the role of England coach. The reason he may leave is nothing to do with the players, or with the team's performance. It is purely to do with the politics of the job and the interference of the RFU, the people who are pulling the strings above him. Does he still want to put up with the hassle? That's the question. It doesn't seem to interfere with his day-to-day coaching role, but he is continually aware of influential people sitting on his shoulder waiting for him to make mistakes. And they have been quick to come forward and indicate that if he does make a mistake he will have to go. It's pretty tough to cope with that all the time, and yet, I suppose, in some respects that's the way in which he treats his players! In some ways, then, it's like giving him a taste of his own medicine. But with a handful of the characters at the RFU it has become more personal, and that would never happen between Jack Rowell and one of his players. Being dropped is never a personal thing; it is purely a playing decision.

It's a tough call for Jack, but I hope that he'll play on and take us into the next World Cup in 1999. He has the talent to take the England team all the way next time round, and he has the full support of the players. If we are ever to reach that ultimate rugby goal, stability and continuity in terms of the coaching staff is vital. I would therefore like to see all of our coaching staff offered some form of job security, perhaps a three-year contract. If Jack stays, then he, more than anyone else, should be given the comfort of a longer term contract rather than working from season to season as specified by his current one-year agreement, which can only be renewed at the behest of the RFU committee. That's ridiculous, and does not lend itself to the team achieving any ambitious long-term goal.

Admittedly, three years is a long commitment to give a coach in the pressure-cooker environment of professional rugby, because the squeeze will always be on to perform. How many top soccer bosses last that long? But supporters, and the RFU, should not overreact when occasional matches are won or lost. We all need to keep a sense of proportion. International rugby is now so competitive that we are going to lose games. What we need to do is to keep things in perspective and work to a common long-term goal, the 1999

World Cup. We can only do that with a settled management team. Jack's position is in stark contrast to Brian Ashton's at Ireland. They have realised the value of continuity and given Brian a six-year contract to take him through the next two World Cups. It is a massive vote of confidence.

I get on well with Jack but he's not someone I would ever ring up to ask whether he fancied nipping out for a quick beer. That's not the sort of relationship we have. I wouldn't describe it as cosy by any stretch of the imagination. It's a working relationship, and just that. He very rarely opens up to me or anyone else even after all this time – unless he's had ten bottles of champagne, that is! On the occasions we have met up with him 'chez Rowell', he is more relaxed among his family, but you are still never really sure what he is thinking.

We go back a long way, of course. We can be straight with each other and that's a good, healthy thing. If something needs saying then I'll say it. I won't hesitate to tell Jack my thoughts, and vice versa. It's a very clean and direct relationship. For instance, I had words with him after the Australia game in the 1995 World Cup. I'd played the two group games against Italy and Western Samoa and I thought that I had played pretty well, and at that time Jerry wasn't playing very well at all. But Jack nevertheless picked him instead of me for the quarter-final against the Wallabies and I was very upset. I bit my tongue for a while, but after our victory we went to celebrate in the Bertie's Landing bar in Cape Town's Waterfront area, and we all got horribly drunk – and me more than most! I launched into Jack, calling him a chicken for not picking me for the quarter-final. He took it well, and appreciated that I was upset (as well as drunk). It probably didn't matter one way or the other, because although he didn't pick me for the rest of the time we were out there, it didn't stop me from later getting my chance as a player and as a captain.

In comparison with the early days in Bath Jack is probably now a bit more intense, but that's not surprising. There is now a lot more pressure on him to get results, and he is playing on the international stage. Lifestyles have also changed. Once upon a time he was working part-time for Dalgety plc and travelling down to Bath for evening training; then he was merely indulging in a passionate hobby. In those days rugby was a release, but you can't treat rugby like that any more. It's a business. Luckily for Jack his wife Sue is a great lady, and she must be very understanding. Certainly she's the nicer partner! What he hasn't got she more than makes up for. I expect that she has probably got used to him by now, in the same way as I expect Yolanda to get used to me too!

POSTSCRIPT

Jack announced that he would not be standing again for the position of England coach five days before the RFU were due to announce his re-appointment, at the end of August 1997. Following the public airing of the quest to get Ian McGeechan to do the job, and McGeechan's subsequent rejection of the offer, Jack's timing was perfect to leave the RFU with egg on their faces. Nobody should be subjected to that sort of behaviour, particularly a coach as successful as Jack had been. I wish him well.

CHAPTER SEVEN

Blood, Sweat and Tears

There was never any need for me to turn up the heat on the players coming into my first Five Nations Championship as captain; it was quite hot enough! International rugby players are a highly motivated bunch of guys these days, otherwise they would not deserve their places. And after the disappointing match against Argentina at Twickenham in mid-December, the pressure was really on the team to go out and perform in the Five Nations.

The dressing-room had not been a happy place after that contest, even though we had scraped a win against the Pumas in a performance which was undoubtedly well below par. Our shape and continuity in the game were both poor, but that's how it goes sometimes. It's the nature of sport to have bad games sometimes; it's how you react to those bad games that counts. You have to move on and adapt to the ever-changing circumstances. The measure of any team is how it copes with adversity, and having agonised on the Argentina display throughout the Christmas period, the Calcutta Cup match was our first chance to show our hardened resolve and fighting spirit.

It was a long six-week wait for the game against the Scots, and during that time there was enormous speculation and media interest about the team line-up and England's intended approach to the tournament. All eyes were on the slightly changed England XV for that first match of the campaign, and we approached the 114th 'old firm' Calcutta Cup clash with some eagerness, not to mention trepidation, having sat out the first round of the tournament.

Even before the championship began I felt it would be a very even contest. There wasn't one side on a roll, and we'd all had the odd hiccup along the way. I did feel, however, that Wales were the most improved team of the five, and that their former rugby league stars had made a big difference. Even before we had set foot on Welsh territory, I did not expect our last game in Cardiff to be much fun!

There are some people who question the quality of play in the Five Nations Championship, and there are even those who see it as a second-rate competition, but to me it is still one of the great highlights in the rugby year. Expectations are always high before the first game, and players as well as supporters invariably get quite a buzz all the way through. The tournament is rich in tradition and means so much to everyone involved.

I had been looking forward to the Five Nations for some time because I thought it was an opportunity for northern hemisphere rugby to show itself to the sporting world in the best possible light. I believe that the games are always of a good standard, whatever the critics say. Of course we want to play the southern hemisphere countries more often, and yes, the standard of their tri-nations series is probably higher. But if one of those countries were immersed in the cauldron of the Five Nations year in, year out, I doubt whether they would fare as well as they do in one-off 'friendly' games against us. The media scrutiny, the public interest and the sense of history all ensure that the intensity of the matches is always far greater than in most other international games.

The matches are always so tense and so furiously contested that it is difficult to stick to your long-term goals. But we had to, not out of slavish devotion to some lofty ambition, but simply because we felt it was the most effective way to play. I did not want to see us retreat into a shell, but neither did I want us to play wild, unstructured rugby. There had to be a balance between the passing and the kicking game. We couldn't go on to the field with too many preconceived notions. We had an outline, of course, as to what we might do, but no more than that. We planned to play integrated, constructive rugby. The forwards had been going reasonably well in the run-in to the match and we felt that it was up to us to try and kick-start the three-quarters. That was the game plan.

I must admit that I was feeling the pressure in the build-up. I felt very tense, and that's not like me. I like to stay as relaxed as possible, and to save all the nervous energy for the game itself. Jack had not helped. He gave me a typical Rowell kick up the backside by asking me whether I should be selected to play, as Jerry Guscott was pressing hard for a place. That was despite the fact that I had put in some decent international performances. I thought my games before Christmas had been quite good, even though I had missed out on the international against Argentina through injury. I was back to my sharpest after Christmas, in good time for the Five Nations.

Admittedly it took me a while to get back into the swing of international rugby. I think some people conveniently forgot that I had only just started playing internationals again after three years of largely sitting on the bench. I had sat on the sideline more than 20 times, and you always need a few games under your belt to recapture your sharpness at this level. In fact, thanks to my limited time on the pitch, I didn't score my first try until the game against South Africa in November 1995 when I came on for skipper Will Carling (it makes a change to get a pass from Catty!). But going into the 1997 Five Nations I felt good and I was determined to make the most of my place in the starting line-up and of being captain. With Jerry challenging hard I didn't feel cosy about my England place, but I certainly didn't feel as though I ought to make way for him. Jack must have felt the same. He knew I was getting back to my best.

Jack too was under pressure. A few weeks before the game, rumours started flying around that he was about to be sacked. There was a lot of truth in the reports that the RFU had been meeting and arguing about Jack's position. They claimed they were talking through 'what if' scenarios, but it certainly undermined the man at an important time. He needed to be thinking through some of the complex selection decisions still to be made, the combinations of players in midfield, at half-back and in the back row. He did not need to be sidetracked into thinking about his international future, then being debated at the hands of the administrators.

Jack's team selections had already prompted Dick Best to deliver a verbal lashing before the friendly against Italy in November, and

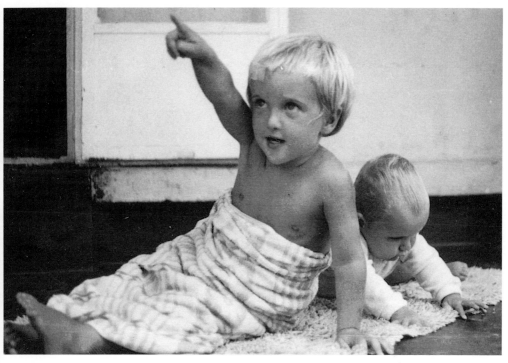

Even as a young man I had a knack for giving directions,
although as usual my sister is not taking any notice!

Without ever pushing me or creating pressure, my parents have had a
significant influence on my career, and I was proud to celebrate Bath's
Courage League Championship with my father

At Bath we'll try any new ideas for training routines – including army camp – once! (© The Western Morning News Co. Ltd)

Local derbies against our old rivals Gloucester are always fiercely contested, and it's not easy to find a way through (© *Bath Chronicle*)

Playing for England requires 100 per cent effort – and celebrating Grand Slams needs to be done properly too!

The World Cup in South Africa was a marvellous experience, and even if we came up a little short of our ambitions, we still played some pretty good rugby – and I had the chance to practise a couple of my favourite summer sports
(© Eddie Keogh)

The most exciting moment of my rugby
career, when I was announced as the new
England captain (© Allsport)

Scoring tries for England is a
great thrill; scoring when
you're the captain just adds
to the pleasure! (© *Bath
Chronicle*)

The happiest day of my life. It beats rugby any way you look at it!
(© Tim Smith Photography)

before the Scotland game Best's England coaching partner Geoff Cooke accused his successor of talking 'mumbo-jumbo'. I really don't know why they were trying to push for the cracks, cracks that didn't exist, with just two or three days to go before a major international. They must have known that it would be disruptive. I hit back on Jack's behalf, commenting that we were 'perfectly clear' as to how the coach wanted us to play and that everything he said made sense, both to me and to the rest of the squad. The message to everyone was that the team was completely behind Jack; it was as simple as that.

As well as the critics in the press (and Jack's critics in the RFU) there is a paying public to satisfy, and if the Twickenham crowd aren't happy then we soon know about it. That's why I also took the opportunity before the game to make a stand against one of the more recent trends among the Twickenham crowd: to hiss, boo and whistle any decision to kick for goal rather than run the ball. I told the newspapers that international rugby is now all about winning and accumulating points at every opportunity. I said that if we were awarded a penalty within range against the Scots, we'd kick it. What's more, I told them that I expected that true rugby supporters would understand. No one remembers the style of a performance five years down the line, but they do remember the final result. I was making a point. Having said that, standards had markedly risen in the club game and I wanted them to apply to the forthcoming Five Nations. I didn't want us to play in a strait-jacket just because it was the Five Nations.

All of this banter and criticism goes with the territory. If we want to play at this level then we simply have to accept it, warts and all. Most of the criticism you can deal with quite comfortably. My only real concern going into the Calcutta Cup game was for the young players, who were not used to this sort of pressure. I had a quiet word with them. I wanted all of them to carry on believing in themselves and not to take any notice of the press critics, because, at this level, confidence is everything. You have to have faith in yourself and those around you. If you don't have that, although you may get away with it in an easy match, in the tight corners you'll be found out – and those tight corners are everywhere in the Five Nations. Self-belief is an intangible quality but it has a real impact on performance.

During the period before the Scotland game it was actually Jerry Guscott who gave me the most useful piece of advice. He told me to forget about being the captain and to just play like a centre. That was a good call, and as I began to play better and better in my own position, I got more comfortable with the pressures and decision-making of the England captaincy. It also showed Jerry for what he really is: an outstanding squad member. I felt it was hard on Jerry to have to sit on the bench again for this game, but with Will playing so well it was only right that he should start his tenth successive Five Nations campaign. I know how difficult it is to be on the bench – I've done it enough times! It's very frustrating, and everyone has their own way of dealing with it. But you only find out the true quality of the player – and also of the person – by how he reacts when he sits on the bench, and Jerry has been superb. He still wants to get involved, and he's always full of advice for other players. Although he's on the touchline, he's still thinking carefully about how we should play the game, and he's still very much part of what's going on. I know how much he wants to be in the team, and, because of that, his contribution has been all the more immense. He will be back soon, and no doubt with a vengeance!

Despite the jangling nerves in the camp, we had a very good training session on the Wednesday before the Scotland game and everyone felt good. It really helped boost the confidence of the squad again after the Argentina game. Everything at that training session felt good and was done at pace. It was great.

We also changed the training format on the day before the game. Tim Rodber suggested that we should try and train at Twickenham, so instead of going down for a team run at the Bank of England ground at a time when everyone would be getting a bit edgy about the game, we went to Twickenham, and it was fantastic. We jogged a few laps of the pitch, then went to the gym for some stretching and flexibility exercises and turned the volume on the CD player up to maximum. We worked out in the gym for about half an hour and then went outside, where the forwards practised some lineouts and the backs did some kicking. It worked, and it certainly eased some of the tension. The younger players also had a chance to get more accustomed to Twickenham. By the time the Saturday came we all felt much better, and that little change in the training routine probably counted for a lot.

Yolanda had recorded a tape for me to listen to before the first Five Nations game but I had forgotten to take my Walkman, so I had to go and listen to it in my car which was parked in the hotel car park. Catty was walking by and must have wondered what was going on, but when he saw it was me he got in and listened. Some of my favourites were on there, including Meatloaf's 'Bat out of Hell', and we began singing along at the tops of our voices. Anyone walking past must have thought we were a couple of nutters!

We made every effort to try and relax throughout the championship. Although I'm a real backgammon fan (and have taken a lot of money off Mr Catt and John Mallett over the years), we tend to play cards while preparing for England games. Backgammon is always more of a favourite on tour. There was a lot of cards played during the Five Nations. Every time we were on the coach – even on the way to training – I seemed to be playing seven-card brag with Ben, Andy Gomarsall, Austin Healey, Alex King and Catty. It was seven-card brag on the coach, and then three-card brag on the Thursday or Friday nights before the game. Jack always told us we had to be in bed by 11 p.m. but you've got to hang in there when you're down, and try to win your cash back even though you know that you're going to lose even more.

As for other 'stress-busters' during the build-up you can never find something that everybody wants to do, although golf and Quasar are popular. I am against forcing anyone to attend 'formal recreation' against their will, but we always go for a team meal on a Wednesday, usually to a little place called Chequers near the hotel in Marlow. We have a meal and a glass of wine, if only to get away from the confines of the hotel. It all helps.

Scotland had not beaten us at Twickenham since 1983 and would clearly be wound up for the battle, so we needed a good start. With

Northampton's Paul Grayson coming into the team at number ten after a period shadowing Mike Catt, and Saracens' Richard Hill in the XV as open-side flanker, we needed to settle and score early to regain some of the surging confidence we had shown earlier in the season. It was far from being one of the dour, forward-dominated Calcutta Cup battles of the past. So untypical was it that the game produced five tries, three in the last quarter of an hour, and we came away victors by 41–13. It was England's record eighth successive win over the hapless Scots – a great way for us to begin our campaign. I was delighted.

We put points on the board fairly early but in 'the most controversial of circumstances' – according to the Scots – when the ref awarded us a penalty try for persistent infringement, having already disallowed a potential Rob Wainwright try. One or two people thought the penalty try was a harsh decision by New Zealand referee Paddy O'Brien, but he had warned us before the game that he would penalise persistent offending, and he was as good as his word. I thought it was a good decision. It marked our first try against the Scots for four years, and broke the deadlock.

But, although we looked quite comfortable, we didn't make the advantage tell, and some sloppy tackling let the Scots in for a try. We ended up going into half-time only 16–10 ahead. The press said that we took 60 minutes to 'soften them up' and then ran in a stack of tries, but in truth the game just happened like that. Near the end the Scots were in tatters, and we began to take them apart. Mick Cleary in the *Observer* said that we 'bristled with intent, pace and guile' from the 60th minute on. 'England stopped talking a good game and started playing one. It was a remarkable transformation,' he added.

After kicking two penalties soon after the break, it all started to come together. Will Carling became more and more conspicuous, and hammered into a position near the Scotland twenty-two. The ruck looked unthreatening until Martin Johnson peeled away and found Andy Gomarsall inside. The Wasps scrum-half nipped over the line. Three minutes later, a sequence of England moves ended with the Scottish defence spread, Tim Rodber found Will with a lobbed pass, and my predecessor as captain made no mistake. He played superbly, even better than his best while he was skipper. It was just one minute later when I did the honours after a break by Paul Grayson, beating Brian Redpath to score my first try in the Five Nations. It was our joint biggest ever win in the championship, equalling our 41–13 victory over France way back in 1907. The rout was complete.

One moment that I particularly recall was racing back to catch and tackle Tony Stanger in a dangerous situation, although I didn't think it was politic to bring that up in my later meeting with Lions boss Fran Cotton, when he said that one of the reasons I had not been selected for the trip to South Africa was my lack of pace. Nonsense. I can't be that slow if I can catch Stanger from behind!

It was a really good all-round performance, and we showed better balance than we had done for some time. We had power up front and speed among the backs; it was a pleasure to play with them. Perhaps we were a little over-keen at the start of the game - it may have been a hangover from the Pumas match – but in the end we could have scored a couple of tries more. And it was great for me to score . . . about time too! The result was a tremendous start to our Five Nations campaign. We had built on the good play in the games against Italy and the New Zealand Barbarians, and we were generally pretty satisfied. We could have had more points as well. Late in the second half we opted not to take some penalty kicks at goal, and we might have had a fifth try in the end. But points were not what it was all about once we had established a valuable cushion. We wanted to establish a style and it was important to keep the momentum going when we were on top.

After our last international against Argentina there had been boos ringing around the stadium. This time we heard 'Swing Low, Sweet Chariot' resounding around the ground and that was wonderful for the players. Jack said, 'It was stop-start for a while but then we managed to dust off the cobwebs. We came out of the psychological bondage. I was delighted with the flow and how we took the opportunities.'

We nevertheless knew that we had to start from scratch for the game against Ireland a fortnight later. It would be another tough encounter, particularly after their win in Cardiff. I thought that we had got the balance right between strength and speed in key areas in the Calcutta Cup game, so I didn't envisage any changes – injuries permitting. It was also entertaining for people to watch, and the win had taken some of the pressure off. We still realised that we had a lot of work to do and there were improvements to be made, but we had shown that once we cut loose, we can play a flowing game that few sides can live with.

The game against the Irish in Dublin was billed as a head-to-head of the two former Bath men, Rowell and Ashton. Jack had brought the Lancastrian Brian Ashton to Bath in 1989, and together they had dominated English club rugby. Now they pitted their wits against each other in the international arena, although Brian had been given precious little time in which to influence the men in green. But in next to no time he had already somewhat revived flagging Irish fortunes – the Irish had beaten the Welsh 26–25 in the previous round of games – and turned a losing team into a winning one. And no opposition coach in the championship could match his detailed knowledge of the England players; he would have worked out all our strengths and weaknesses. It was always going to be a tough proposition, and with Brian now in charge of the Irish team it was set to be even tougher. I felt it was going to turn out to be a battle of wits. How ironic that a coach from whom I had learned so much in his years at Bath should now be doing his level best to ensure my England side fell flat on its face.

Having sat through England's last two matches at Lansdowne Road, I knew what to expect. Playing against Ireland is like no other game because of the sheer fury it generates. We were ready and waiting for a lot of ferocious hits. Once again we had to weigh in with 60 minutes of hard graft, and then we ran away with the game 46–6 in just the same way as we had done against the Scots to produce another record-breaking score. We didn't set out intending to 'soften the Irish up', it simply looked like it. But we did get more confident during the latter stages, as we had done in the game against Scotland, and it was then that we started to throw the ball about more.

There was, perhaps, one crucial moment that went our way. The Irish winger Hickie stepped inside and slipped on the bumpy turf when he was clear and probably would have scored. At that point the game was still quite tight and evenly balanced. That could have made a big difference, and in terms of confidence it was during a key period of the game. In fact, twice early on the Irish made our defence creak. It was stop–start and we did make some mistakes under pressure. Certainly we were undisciplined in the first half, and we gave away far too many penalties. In hindsight, we felt it was one of the areas which we still needed to work on and tighten up. I spent a lot of the game tackling. We knew they'd come at us very hard and we were right.

At half-time we led 11–6, thanks to a try in the corner from Jon Sleightholme courtesy of Tony Underwood and myself. However, once we stepped up a gear in the second half, with the wind at our backs, we were unstoppable. A try from Andy Gomarsall opened the floodgates. Andy began the scoring by slipping through courtesy of a dummy to the blind side of a five-metre scrum, and then Ireland appeared to self-destruct at 24–6. We scored four tries in the last eight minutes through Sleights again, Richard Hill and two from Tony Underwood, the last a magnificent running effort with almost the whole team involved. As soon as we got some space we ran beautiful lines. In fact, we started to pull so far ahead so quickly that Jack brought on Austin Healey for a first cap, and Jerry Guscott for three dazzling and very productive minutes.

I felt good after that game. Most of the journos were saying that if we continued like this we could break all Five Nations records, but despite the impressive victory there was still some criticism being levelled at the England team concerning the 'imprecision' of our play. Some of the critics argued that if we had been playing a better team we would have been punished. That may have been so but it undermined our performance, which I felt had been another huge step in the right direction.

Gradually the England team was coming together on the pitch. We were playing better and the key combinations, like the back row, were also coming to understand each other. Tim Rodber played especially well – I don't think that I had seen him play like that in an England shirt for a long time – and Tony Underwood may have had his best ever international game. You often have a purple patch in a game, a spell where everything starts going right. Now we have to try and put four of our 20-minute purple patches into just one which is 80 minutes long! An excellent prospect.

Whereas we rammed home our advantage in the last 20 minutes of the games against Scotland and Ireland, the wheels came off in the last quarter against France – the low point of my season. Having led 20–6 after an hour, and having begun to play the kind of expansive, integrated game that we had so often talked about, and all in front of an appreciative home crowd, it all went horribly wrong and we were beaten by three points, the final score 20–23.

There is never any need to get the team 'up' for an encounter against the French, and we went into the match at Twickenham quiet, calm and pretty well focused, although I did have a few stern words to say at the meeting on the Friday night before the game as I didn't feel that some of the side were quite in tune mentally. But there was nothing wrong with the build-up. We were not over-confident despite the euphoria of the two big victories preceding this match, and there was no shortfall of passion to take on the French. Between 1989 and 1995 France had lost every game against England, but the run was broken in Pretoria in South Africa during the World Cup when France beat us in a lacklustre third-place play-off. The French also won the Five Nations match in 1996. So the balance of power had shifted over the last two years, and we desperately wanted to redress the balance in our favour.

I did not need to rant and rave in the dressing-room beforehand. We knew there was a job to be done. There was a noticeably quieter atmosphere around the England dressing-room in the build-up to this year's game against France, with no Brian Moore to bait the opposition. Brian always played with passion and desire in his England shirt and his influence was enormous, but he invariably baited the opposition and there was occasionally some ugliness as a result. Nowadays, players like Jason Leonard and Mark Regan prefer to do most of their talking on the field rather than off it, although in private they undoubtedly feel just as passionate. The rivalry between the French and the English is intense and it was always going to be a physical, passionate encounter, but we hoped that there would not be any of the nastiness there had been in previous meetings.

We felt that the French needed to be hit hard and early, up front and by the backs. We also thought that there would be fewer points-scoring opportunities than against Scotland and Ireland, so we knew that we had to be as clinical as we could be in taking anything that came our way. We knew that the French would inevitably cross our gain line, and that we had to find a way to strangle their potential to run at us. We had to give them something to think about, and for the first hour we did that and more. But experience should have told us that the French are always dangerous and that you can never relax in any area of the pitch, not for one moment. The first big play came on the stroke of half-time with England already leading 9–6 and playing well. We had made great strides by giving the ball to our running back row and it was Richard Hill who made the initial burst and gave the ball to me. I turned it inside to Lawrence Dallaglio who made a burst through the cover and scored. That made it 14–6 at half-time.

When France went 20–6 down, I felt that they had graciously accepted defeat. We were strong and they were nowhere. They had even lost their captain Abdel Benazzi, their one forward who had played the first hour with conviction. If only we had taken a few more of our chances in that period, we would have been out of sight and never in any danger of being caught. One or two missed penalties cost us dear, for the men in blue found new spirit and verve and delivered us a devastating blow, scoring two killer tries in a searing ten-minute spell. Our back row had been so powerful in the first hour. Tim Rodber and Lawrence Dallaglio had been superb. But then we lost control both in the back row and particularly at half-back. We contrived to throw the game away.

We kicked for touch, lost the lineout and they scored immediately with a little chip over the top of Tony Underwood. If he had been able to catch that ball, it probably would have been a completely different story. That was the single defining moment between a Triple Crown and a Grand Slam. It's small things like that which can and often do change whole seasons. However, all credit to the French, who played superbly for the last quarter. They pulled back to level in the 70th minute after a blistering forward drive took us off our own ball. The forwards drove on and good work from Penaud helped send Christophe Lamaison side-stepping his way over our line. He kicked the conversion to make the score 20–20. The suddenly irresistible French won the game in a gripping and desperate finale, thanks to a Lamaison penalty awarded because we killed the ball near our line. Lamaison was outstanding, a match-winner on the day. It was the first French win at Twickenham since 1987, and they could hardly believe it.

I don't think I have ever been in a dressing-room where the players have been so gutted. We were devastated, having expected to win and win well from that commanding half-time lead. We knew only too well that we had thrown away the initiative and along with it the Grand Slam and the Five Nations Championship in just 20 slack minutes. But what disappointed me most was the way we lost the game. We thought we had it in the bag, and relaxed too soon.

This game was different from our first two wins, when we had managed to wear down the opposition and score a flood of points in the last quarter. This time we were unable to maintain our control as time wore on and the tables were turned, although in the end it was very close and we only lost by one penalty. It felt like a kick in the teeth for all the players. There was a sombre mood in our dressing-room that was in stark contrast to the singing in the French changing-rooms. I knew then that it would be a major test of character to get the players 'up' for the difficult game to come against Wales. But this England side deserved not to be written off simply on the basis of one narrow defeat.

Together with the experienced players in the squad I had a major role in helping the youngsters get over this defeat and in analysing where it had gone wrong. In the first half we played some wonderful rugby and created a lot of chances. In fact, we could have easily turned a few more into points and made the game safe. Then we switched off in the second half. When the French came at us we lost our pattern and shape and lost balls that we should have won, although we defended well for much of the match.

The French played their part and Sadourny always looked dangerous, although we managed to stop many of his blind-side moves. Lamaison was superb throughout. He only missed one kick all afternoon, and that hit the post. The French back row also played well as a unit, even after losing their captain and replacing him with a hooker. The critics said that on the day I played probably my best individual England game of the season to date, but my strategic magic wand went AWOL and I could do nothing to stem the French tide. The result would also turn out to be a great disappointment for one other player in particular: it was Will Carling's last international game at Twickenham.

The following week the squad met to talk about each of the first three Five Nations games, but even seven days on from the game against France we did not have any individual feedback and analysis about our own performances. That's an area we have to improve upon in the future. It would help us to realise what we could be doing during a game to improve our contribution. There should be a video plus a critical dossier of everyone's performance game by game. Ironically, although we don't yet do it for the senior England team, I think that Richard Hill does just that with the 'A' team.

Whichever way we looked at it the Grand Slam had gone, but we still had the Triple Crown to play for. But Wales were going to be a very difficult side to beat. They would now be fired up and ready to attack like demons on our visit. The Arms Park promised to be a cauldron, and we would need to dig deep for a massive final effort. We had been given a lesson by the French and I hoped that we could learn from our mistakes. Jack Rowell also gave us the opportunity. He immediately made it clear that there were not likely to be many changes to the side, so the bulk of the team had a chance to make amends.

Our Triple Crown decider against Wales was the last ever game at Cardiff Arms Park, which finally bade farewell to international rugby. If there were Welsh tears for the loss of the Arms Park, worse was to come – tears of real grief as the Red Rose beat the Welsh Dragon 34–13 to win the Triple Crown, and by yet another record score. It was our biggest ever win at this stadium where we have traditionally struggled. It was sweet.

On the Saturday just before the Welsh game I probably said more than I had before any of the other Five Nations fixtures. I like to have the team together for that last ten minutes before we run out on to the pitch. I asked them to play 'with arrogance' and to try and make the big emotional occasion work for us as much as it would work for them. I said, 'Let's not go out there to win by a point. Let's stuff them because we know we can do it!' The Welsh had been mouthing off beforehand about how England were 'so boring' and how we never ever scored tries against them. So our objective was to keep the Welsh crowd quiet for as much of the match as possible, and to make them go home early.

The atmosphere at Cardiff Arms Park was extraordinary, and very emotional. We particularly enjoyed the playing of the anthems that day, one of the only moments in any big game where you are really aware of the closeness of the crowd. You often find yourself humming along to the other anthems – I certainly remember humming 'The Flower of Scotland' in the game at Twickenham! You can't help it, because they're all good tunes. The wall of noise at the Arms Park for that final game was an awesome din, but rather than feeling intimidated by the Welsh passion and fervour, it helped to lift us. The intensity of that keyed-up Welsh home crowd seemed to give everyone an added boost, even though they were cheering for the Welsh team, and the result was great. It was a really upbeat way to end a hard Five Nations campaign.

Wales found it difficult to cope with a handful of injuries before the game, and when Neil Jenkins and Christian Loader had to leave the field during the match it was the final nail in their coffin. Nevertheless, our defence was impeccable and we played well. We got the balance just right. With so much confidence now evident, the team weren't just talking about enterprising rugby, we were playing it. We pledged to be ruthless this time round if we found ourselves anything like 20–6 up, as we had been against France.

And, amazingly, we went 20–6 up again. This time, however, we dug in and scored two clinching tries. It was very satisfying.

England had problems in the first half with referee Joel Dume's interpretation of the lineout law. He gave some very strange decisions. We did everything we could to work our way round his rulings, but it took a long time to get used to him. It wasn't until the second half that we found a way round it, the forwards having adjusted magnificently to his interpretation.

After half-time we started to throw the ball wide and, once again, we managed to find a fluid and effective rhythm. But for having a try disallowed late on, we could have had 40 points on the board by the final whistle. Jerry Guscott's super mazy jinking run sent Richard Hill clear for the third try and Catty did the business for me to score again, which helped make the day special. We took a quick tap penalty, Catty shot through a gap, and it was a case of me being in the right place at the right time. He also kicked well in his best international game of the season. When he came off he was smiling like a 'Cheshire Catt' – and so too was his surprise replacement Rob Andrew, who won his 71st cap.

We haven't really got into the habit of using substitutes. We hacked on about that to Jack all the way through last season. He eventually began using subs and brought on Rob in that last game, but it didn't come easily. It wasn't in Jack's rugby culture and he didn't like doing it because he was worried about the impact it would have on the players being brought off. However, I reckon that those same players are generally quite happy to play 60 or 70 minutes and then be replaced by someone with fresh legs who will bust a gut for the last period, particularly if they have played well.

A few pundits were saying that the Welsh game was the last chance for me to impress the Lions tour manager Fran Cotton, but I'm sure that he already knew who his final squad would be and I wasn't going to be in it. The game may have been billed as such, but as far as I was concerned it was never about proving a point to Cotton. It was about Wales versus England, and making sure our team came out on top.

The game saw the final international appearances of two players who have been great servants for England, Will Carling and Rob Andrew. Both of them can be immensely proud of their contribution to international rugby over the last decade, and both will be able to reflect on some wonderful memories and some magnificent England performances. And, thanks to Will, the current crop of young players now know what the reward is for totting up more than 70 caps: he was presented with a silk tie rather than one of the polyester ones we get!

If the game marked the end for key senior players, it also gave a few newcomers the chance to make their mark. Phil Greening came on at half-time for only his second appearance and had a good game – he will be a star in the future – and Darren Garforth won his first cap in what was a special occasion for him, although I'm sure he would have liked to have been on a bit longer.

Had it not been for the final quarter against France we would have won the Grand Slam in amazing style. Alas, the dream slipped through our fingers. And yet I feel the best is yet to come. We have now moved on and we will only get better and better. The signs were all there during the Five Nations games, and the prospects are genuinely exciting, giving us great heart and confidence for the future. Playing expansive, integrated, 15-man rugby as we have done at times only comes with confidence, and now the whole squad is bubbling. We are not only winning but we are playing rugby with style.

Indeed, the style of our games in the 1996–97 season was streets ahead of where we were the year before, yet most of the rugby writers failed to pick up on that. Nobody stood back and looked at the wider perspective, the whole season, which would have highlighted the fact that England played well and actually went places. It's somewhat irksome because the team developed so much over the season. In fact, it took someone like François Pienaar to give England a slap on the back. He was in tune with what we were trying to achieve, and yet the rugby journos seemed to miss it. As a team we deserved more credit than they gave us. If we can maintain that confidence and continue to develop at the same pace, I am sure we'll give the All Blacks, Springboks and Wallabies a hard time when they come to Twickenham later in 1997. My job now is to try and get the balance right between playing positive rugby and ensuring we don't make mistakes. It's still a challenge we have to meet.

I shared a bottle of wine with Catty after the Wales game in the Five Nations and what he said was a real boost to my own confidence. He said some really kind things to me, such as 'Well done, and congratulations for coping with the pressure, both as a player and as a captain.' It meant a lot to me, especially coming from one of my close England teammates.

I must admit it felt good to get off the bench and play last year. I had been brought on quite often as a replacement in the past, as I had been covering a number of positions for injury, but there's nothing like being in the starting line-up and in the thick of the action after serving such a lengthy apprenticeship. I played well against France and Wales, but I didn't have too much to do against Scotland and Ireland, although I scored in the Calcutta Cup game. All in all I was very happy with my performances.

Across the whole championship a number of new talents emerged. Mark 'Ronnie' Regan had a terrific Five Nations, as did Simon Shaw. Richard Hill made the position of open-side flanker his own, and he was probably the most consistent England player of the season. Tim Stimpson got better and better at full-back, despite having been under pressure early on. Apart from a rough 20 minutes against France, Paul Grayson had a good season, and my fellow centre Will Carling played superbly against Scotland.

But there are still some positions up for grabs. Andy Gomarsall did well up until Christmas but then his game started to go as the pressure began to mount, and Austin Healey came into the side as his replacement. Austin is incredibly cocky and a very good player. He did all the right things against Wales, and didn't take on too much too quickly. He is also a fine cover tackler, and he will be a good player in years to come, but he may have a few problems because he is so cocky and arrogant. He may find it difficult to fit into some teams.

The great thing from the England point of view is that the squad is young, and therefore it is quite likely to remain settled. It gives us every chance coming into the 1999 Rugby World Cup. Throughout the Five Nations I felt that our forwards were magnificent, and they not only showed terrific understanding between each other, they also instinctively knew what to do with the ball. They may not yet be on a par with their colleagues in the southern hemisphere, but they're certainly getting there. The front five in particular played like a real unit. In fact they could be related, as they tend to roam around together both on and off the pitch, in contrast to the 'individuals' in the side, the boys in the back row and the backs.

Psychologically there is a significant difference between the characters in the squad. On the one hand you have people like Austin Healey, a man who loves to abuse everyone all of the time, and 'Ronnie' Regan, the team's Bristolian joker. For some unknown reason 'Ronnie' just loves playing completely daft and utterly pointless games, but he still manages to make us laugh. On the other hand there are the quieter players, brooding giants like Simon Shaw and Martin Johnson. Martin, in particular, is very hard to talk to, and I feel that he doesn't always relax and enjoy engaging in conversation. Martin's not at all hard to motivate but he is certainly hard to judge. It was fascinating to see how he led the Lions.

Generally the squad had a good balance to it during the 1996–97 season, and judging by the amount of abuse I got from the lads – a good barometer of relationships and team spirit – I think the other players were comfortable with me both as an England teammate and captain.

Giving and taking stick is what rugby is all about, and that's the way it works at Bath too. I remember one occasion where I took a lot of grief from the lads because I missed a Tuesday-afternoon training session, followed by one on the Thursday. Immediately they picked up on my absence and I was re-nicknamed 'Bernard', as in Bernard Gallagher – a non-playing captain. To use more golfing jargon, that's par for the course. In rugby there are no hiding-places. It's a tough and demanding environment, and you have to learn to live with it.

After the game against Wales the England team just broke up, without a 'debriefing', and the next time we planned to come together was for the tour to Argentina. When we finally got together for our first session, however, we only had 13 fit players out of the 30-man squad, so we had to be content with watching a few old Pumas videos. There was just one further pre-tour build-up session planned, to take place one Wednesday at Bisham Abbey, followed by a meeting-cum-training session on the Saturday and Sunday prior to travelling on the Monday. The flight lasted around 24 hours and we went straight into a big midweek game against the provincial champions.

All of that could hardly be regarded as good preparation resulting from competent planning, and neither could a three-week tour to Argentina followed by three weeks at home (just long enough to 'soften up' physically) and then a hard ten-day tour down under. And all followed closely by perhaps the longest, hardest and most physical domestic, European and international season ever played. Surely it would have been more sensible to tie the Argentinian and Australian trips in together? If I had been one of the administrators in charge I would probably have omitted the short tour to Australia or put Argentina in the diary a little later so that we could fly on to Oz on the way home. As it was it became a very bitty summer for us, although I concede there was little or no flexibilty as the Aussies were already involved in so many games.

It smacked of a general absence of good planning, which goes hand in hand with a lack of administrative and managerial support in key areas, deficiencies which still plague the England team. These are areas in which we have to improve in order to enable us to compete with the best. In particular, the England team needs more back-up at international level. For instance, we need a proper administrative manager who can sort out the basics, including simple things like the team's hotel and meeting rooms. On the Saturday morning of our Five Nations game against Wales our England team room at the hotel in Cardiff was being used for corporate hospitality. That meant we had to go down into a horrible old room by the kitchens for breakfast during what was a critical time for the players in the final run-in to a major international. We were then put into another room for the team meeting before we left for the game. It was ridiculous, and yet there was nobody within the management empowered to sort it out on our behalf. This is only one example of something that could easily have been avoided, but it helps to illustrate how the England team needs more professional back-up. It needs to be improved, for, make no mistake, it really is important.

However, our existing back-room team did a fine job in 1996–97, and they deserve a great deal of credit. Many of them are unsung heroes. That team is crucial to the well-being of the players, and includes guys like 'Smurf' (Kevin Murphy), 'the Doctor' (Terry Crystal), and Richard Wegrzyk, the masseur. The role of these people should never be underestimated, for they can often gauge the 'temperature' of the squad better than anyone else.

The coaching management was also good, with Jack as head coach and Les Cusworth and Mike Slemen ('Slem') as assistant coach and selector respectively. 'Slem' usually works with the back three, Les with the backs and Jack with the forwards, so we all tend to get some individual attention. I have some input with Les as far as the backs are concerned, although I often seem to spend more time trying to rein in Jack's enthusiasm and keep him to schedule. More typical would be me shouting, 'Right, Jack, this really is the last scrum, the very last, and then we're back to the hotel.' (Jack can have you out there for a long time if you don't bully him a little!)

But even though the coaching worked out well, some of the overall administration and planning was shocking. For example, if the RFU told kicking coach Simon Hodgkinson to turn up at 10.30 a.m. for kicking practice, we were inevitably midway through a full squad session. That meant he had to wait around to do the kicking afterwards, by which time we were all knackered. Simon had effectively wasted a trip through no fault of his own. It wasn't unusual, and that sort of bad planning has got to be improved tenfold in the future.

We are still very amateur in terms of preparation off the pitch. We now see match videos of our opponents, with key plays broken down and analysed. But we still need an individual video review of our own performance after a game, and the input of rugby experts who can sit down and talk us through the good and the bad moments, along with the missed opportunities. It's only then that we can really improve as individuals. None of that happens at the moment.

Take a look at the professional and well-managed approach of the All Blacks and the differences become obvious. Fran Cotton told me that he had seen the 'Hotel Management Booklet' that the New Zealanders use for going on tour. It's about an inch thick and details the team requirements from what food they are going to have and how it's going to be prepared, right the way through to what the hotel rooms should have in them, and even what sizes the beds should be. It is worked out efficiently and professionally, and in minute detail. We should learn this lesson in professionalism from our friends in the black shirts. To be a winner on the pitch, you need professional support and rock-solid administration behind you, and there is no sensible or justifiable reason why we shouldn't be getting both.

CHAPTER EIGHT

The Lions Roar

'A sweet pass to me and I only had one thing on my mind. At the same time I thought, "What if I miss?" But I didn't, it sailed between the posts, three points, series win, thanks very much.'

LIONS CENTRE JERRY GUSCOTT, AFTER THE 18–15
SECOND TEST VICTORY AT KING'S PARK, DURBAN

When the British Isles triumphed 2–1 in the Test series against South Africa, it gave a sharp reminder to the rugby world that the northern hemisphere game should never be underestimated.

The Lions squad may not have been the most naturally gifted ever to have left our shores, but it gelled together superbly and the team spirit was never in doubt. The planning and preparation done by Fran Cotton and Ian McGeechan was professional from the start and it paid off. Their astute game plan helped to maximise the potential of the Lions, and it was executed to perfection. Our defence was extraordinary throughout the tour, and every chance was taken with relish. As we always suspected he would, Guscott eventually grabbed the international limelight like never before with his sublime drop goal to win the second Test, and Scott Gibbs – the player of the tour – was magnificent, showing huge strength and courage. But the team was full of heroes, typified by the tracer-bullet goal-kicking of Neil Jenkins and the tackling of Lawrence Dallaglio. Even Matt Dawson, thought so lucky by some to have even made the tour, came through with honours, having carved his name in Lions history with a superb individual try. Unlike the Springboks, the Lions never weakened until the series

116

was won. Although I celebrated from afar, I was as proud as anyone. To beat the world champions was everything. Although the 'Boks are perhaps not the side they were in 1995, the Lions winning and winning well in their backyard has sent shock waves through South African rugby.

Even before the Lions squad boarded the plane to Johannesburg, they were acutely aware that the 13-game tour of South Africa was going to be an immense and gruelling sporting challenge, perhaps the biggest of their rugby careers. It was to be the equivalent of ten Five Nations games – against the big, bruising provincial sides eager to soften up the northern hemisphere tourists – and three World Cup finals – against the supremely talented Springboks.

It would be tough, so the team needed to think and act as one from the start. Home-nation rivalries had to be put into suspended animation, and old domestic scores settled with a handshake and a smile. Members of four fiercely competitive teams had to play together as one, making it all the more remarkable that we came through as victors.

As far as I am concerned, I am not ashamed to admit that it would have been a dream come true if I had secured a place on the 24th Lions tour. But, privately, I never thought for one moment that I would be in the final 35-man tour party, even before the selection pool of 62 players was announced during the Five Nations campaign. All of the vibes I'd got from fellow players, from the media and from my very limited contact with Lions tour manager Fran Cotton, indicated that I would not be in the frame this time round, so throughout the 1996–97 season I prepared to go on the England tour of Argentina. I guessed correctly.

Looking back, it seems somewhat odd that, had it not been for injury, I would have made the British Lions tour to New Zealand in 1993, at a time when I was only ever on the England bench. I had been named as a non-travelling reserve for the trip and, when Lion Scott Hastings broke his jaw, I was asked to fly out as a replacement. It was not meant to be. Two days earlier I had dislocated my shoulder joint on the England 'A' tour of Canada.

Four years later it was my dreams that were in pieces rather than my collarbone!

I had initially met Fran Cotton across the huge wooden negotiating table at the East India Club in London, one of the venues for a meeting between EPRUC and the RFU. I was one of the England players' representatives trying to intercede in the already tense negotiations. I think it was the first time that they had sat down properly and tried to get their heads together, but it was doomed from the moment it began. It was a crazy way to try and negotiate. There were too many people involved in the all-day meeting – more than a dozen from each side – and it soon disintegrated into a slanging match. To be frank, it was chaotic.

Even before the meeting began the signs were not encouraging. I knew we were in trouble as soon as the RFU's executive chairman Cliff Brittle insisted on sitting with his back to the window, which he considered to be a 'superior negotiating position'! That set the hostile tone, and drew the battle lines for the day's events.

Fran Cotton was firmly aligned to Cliff Brittle in the meeting, supporting his efforts to bring the clubs to heel. But, contrary to some reports, I didn't clash with Fran as an individual; there was no head-to-head. We were just fighting our opposite corners amid enormous tension. During the meeting Fran was quite vociferous about protecting English rugby, and he outlined his view that divisional rugby is the way forward to protect and enhance the game in the future. That was just one of the arguments, many of which became heated and somewhat aggressive, with the control of the game's finances always at the very top of the different agendas round the table.

Cliff Brittle was very forthright throughout, as was Newcastle's Sir John Hall on behalf of the clubs. It created a lot of antagonism, and, on reflection, clearly wasn't the right way to go about finding any sort of equitable solution. It was like two Sumo wrestlers trying to push each other from the ring, with neither prepared to give an inch. The meeting was altogether too big for its own good, and it was always likely to end in a stand-off.

Because of my active involvement in those negotiations, I suspect that Cliff Brittle may have put me on file in his mind as a potential troublemaker. I also think he wondered what mandate the players had to be at the meeting. But I don't believe Fran Cotton ever felt the same way, even though he was Cliff's ally. There is no doubt, however, that Fran would have walked out of the negotiations harbouring 'negative thoughts' about yours truly. It was inevitable, as we were fighting for opposing sides. But it was never a personal thing between us, and I don't think it had any bearing on my omission from the Lions party. That painful decision ultimately reflected the selectors' judgements about my playing abilities, and Fran was only one of the selectors, albeit the most influential. The selectors *en masse* would have had the same kind of discussions as every other serious rugby fan having a pint with his mates after Christmas, asking, 'Who are the best rugby players in the British Isles?' It was never going to be an easy decision, and tough choices needed to be made.

I think I was good enough to tour, despite the competition for places, and so did many others, including fellow players, rugby writers and supporters. However, it was the collective decision of Fran Cotton and the other selectors that I would not be up to it, and that's what hurt the most. Even though I did not expect to make the final touring party, I had hoped to make the initial squad – which would have been a vindication of both my playing ability and my international performances post-Christmas – but I had never expected to be included just because I was the England skipper. I never thought for one moment that the captaincy would count in my favour, nor would I have wanted it to, and I certainly never expected to go on the tour purely because I wore the captain's armband for England. My omission from the pool of 62 players nevertheless touched a raw nerve, and I felt snubbed as a good player.

A number of elements come into the selection equation at this level, and there's always more to it than just playing ability. It will also depend on whether the selector feels the player is up to the job physically as well as mentally. Character judgement is important. For example, there are plenty of players in the English game who are technically competent and highly skilled. They could play for England, but they are not selected because 'the management' perceives a weakness in another important aspect of their game. Picking a rugby team involves subjective decision-making, and it will always be so. Everybody has a view and inevitably there will be disagreement. No two people think the same. Indeed, if you had asked a dozen different supporters their starting XV for the Lions, you would almost certainly have been faced with 12 different teams.

I heard the news about my omission from the 62-man Lions pool soon after I returned from the England game against Ireland in the Emerald Isle which had resulted in a famous Five Nations victory. Up until then I had been on a massive high. I went to training as usual at 9.30 a.m. on the Monday morning, and the dressing-room jokers were ready and waiting. 'Where are you going to take your summer holidays, Phil?' and 'It looks like it's going to be Argentina for you this summer, DG' were favourites. I wondered what was going on, because I hadn't heard the early-morning news bulletin and still had my mind on the triumph at Lansdowne Road. It didn't take long to find out: the Lions squad had been announced, and I wasn't included. The banter didn't end there, of course. In Bath's next fixture against local rivals Bristol, the crowd joined the bandwagon. 'What are you doing this summer, Phil?' was a pet favourite of the Bristol supporters standing near the halfway line!

My initial reaction was one of both personal disappointment and annoyance, as the timing of the announcement could not have been much worse. Some of my teammates who had also been left out of the squad were devastated, with two games still to play in the Five Nations. Had anyone in the Lions management considered what it would do to the morale of the players who were omitted? With so few Lions tours, selection is priceless. The lads who made it were obviously delighted, and that's great. Equally, the disappointment of losing out on selection could have had a dramatic impact on performance at a crucial time, because confidence is a big part of the battle for players at the highest level. It was bound to unsettle some of the players who were omitted, and it must have been difficult for them to pick themselves up off the floor and refocus in time for them to prove a point in the next Five Nations international, just a few days later. The sense of timing was therefore appalling, and I said as much to the press. Surely it could have waited a few more weeks.

I always knew that this first stage of Lions selection would take place early in the year, but I'd had other more pressing things to think about and didn't expect the news to come during the championship. It was therefore a bolt from the blue. I certainly wasn't waiting for the announcement. The Lions squad was evidently named well in advance so that the potentially difficult contract negotiations could take place, and, admittedly, the date of the announcement was 'in the rugby diary'. But I still found it a bitter pill to swallow at a time when I needed the hearts, minds and souls of my England colleagues to be firmly focused on the French.

Jack Rowell gave myself, Tony Underwood and Jon Sleightholme some paternal advice after the news was announced. 'The best way to earn a place on the Lions tour,' he said, was 'to play well for England in the next two matches'. However, I always harboured grave doubts that my performances in those games would make any difference whatsoever. Jack reckoned that the news would make us more determined to do well in the following games, but personally I didn't need any extra incentive to go out and give my all. Wearing an England shirt and the England captain's armband was more than enough incentive.

Jack nevertheless paid me a very flattering compliment along the way. He compared me to John Dawes, the captain of the 1971 Lions in New Zealand. He said, 'I'm not saying Phil is as good or as bad or whatever as Dawes. But in his own way Phil is the equivalent – and he is getting people to play around him. We're starting to exercise the playing talents we have, and not least some of that, and the tactical direction, is down to Mr de Glanville. That's why he was chosen as England captain.'

The selection door was left ajar by Fran Cotton, and I was pleased that one or two players sneaked into the final 35 even though they were not in the initial pool. But while Neil Back and

Tony Underwood made the touring party thanks to their fine mid-season performances, many other players had their dreams shot to pieces with a lot of the season still to play. However, looking at it from another slightly different perspective, I suppose it could have been a blessing in disguise to have been left out so early on. It must have been far worse for some of the players who made the initial squad, but not the 35-strong touring party.

I always had a sixth sense that I wouldn't make the final line-up, despite having every confidence in my ability. That feeling was based on conversations I'd had with other players and comments in the press. As soon as Allan Bateman and Scott Gibbs began playing well it made it even more difficult, and with Jerry Guscott always a favourite to make his third Lions tour, it made the competition for places very tough.

But when I heard that I had been left out of that starting squad I was upset, and I expected someone from the Lions management to give me a telephone call to soften the blow and explain the decision, at the very least. As far as I know there were no courtesy calls made at all, either to me or any of the other players omitted from either the 62 or the final 35. It was only because the press made an issue of my exclusion that Fran Cotton finally telephoned Bath chief executive Tony Swift to have a chat about the situation. According to Tony, Fran couldn't understand why the media were focusing on players who hadn't made the team, rather than concentrating on the ones who had!

At the same time I let my guard down in public for the one and only time to date, and the press were ready and waiting. I was invited to speak to a group of 50 or 60 students at the Cambridge Union just a few days after the Lions announcement, and I was still acutely disappointed. It was a very informal occasion, and I spent about an hour answering general questions from the floor. I assumed the audience was entirely made up of university students, but there was one canny journalist sharpening his pencil at the back of the room. Then came a question about the Lions selection, and I answered honestly. First of all I said that choosing any rugby team is a subjective decision; it's your personal view about the best players. Secondly, I made the point that the only time I had met Fran was across a very hostile negotiating table, when a lot of harsh words were spoken. We have different views of the game, I said, indicating, perhaps a little too forcibly, that Fran was not necessarily one of my most ardent fans! I was caught out, and the press had a field day.

The furore eventually prompted a lunch between Fran Cotton and myself in Bath at the end of April, a clear-the-air meeting probably instigated by Tony Swift and Bath coach Clive Woodward. I think Clive had said that I was 'a bit hurt', having stepped in and acted as something of an intermediary. I was very happy to talk to Fran after the Five Nations campaign because I felt it would be good for me to get some sort of critical appraisal of my playing ability. I expected nothing more. I wasn't going on the Lions trip, and that was that, despite my slick performances in the last two international games of the season. We had lunch at a little restaurant in Bath, and it was good in terms of smoothing over the problems between us that had been blown out of all proportion in the public arena. And Fran also paid the bill! But I felt that he didn't listen as well as he talked, and I came away from the meeting none the wiser as to the real reasons why I hadn't made the Lions tour party.

Fran threw in a few of the qualities that he was looking for, qualities he clearly felt I did not have. He indicated that my 'lack of pace' had counted against me in selection, highlighting an incident in the last minute of the game against the New Zealand Barbarians when I was caught making a break. I pointed out that it was nothing to do with a lack of pace. I'd picked up a dead leg, and had been hobbling for much of the second half. It even kept me out of the following game against Argentina. But Fran wasn't paying attention – he wasn't interested in listening to my 'lame excuse'. At that stage I backed off – it was a waste of time. So I didn't point out any of the quick breaks that I had made in later games, or the fact that I had caught and tackled the flying Tony Stanger from behind in the Five Nations game against Scotland. It was pointless to argue. Fran had made his decision and, come what may, he would stick by it. Fran also said that he was looking for physical 'presence' in his team, and here too he indicated that I didn't make the Lions grade. But surely it's what happens on the pitch that should count, and I've always felt that my tackling and chasing skills are up there with the best.

Save these few broad brush – and, in my opinion, inappropriate – throwaway comments, there was no specific appraisal of my ability or lack of it, and no encouragement to go away and improve x or y in my game. He didn't want to get too involved in any personal detail. That was disappointing, as I'd expected more feedback. It felt as though he was meeting me because he felt he ought to after the hostile reaction of the press.

The faltering discussion left the way open for us to chat about his views on divisional and European rugby. He's a fan of the divisional approach, I'm a fan of the European game, and there was no meeting-point in between despite the open conversation. Happily, those differences between us don't extend to style. Like me, Fran wants his team to play attractive rugby. That had to be the right way for the Lions to approach and take on the South Africans.

I had no further contact with Fran after that meeting in April. That was disappointing. And I found it even more disappointing that I had no contact whatsoever with Lions coach Ian McGeechan, the man who was apparently the driving force behind the selection of the half-backs and the centres. I know that they all had a great deal to do before the tour, and that I was not a priority. But it would have made such a difference if someone had taken me and a few of the other unlucky players to one side, so that we could have been told exactly why we had been left out. It would also have been good man management, because some of those up-and-coming players will be Lions stars of the future.

Although Martin Johnson was initially one of a number of good captains the Lions could have chosen, his selection was not a surprise. Fran Cotton had always indicated that he was looking for 'power and presence' among his front-line troops, and Martin's name sprung from the list of candidates as the guy who most embodied the Cotton approach: imposing, tough and mean. If there is one man you would want with you in a battle, it's Martin, and clearly Fran Cotton felt the same. It gave 'Johnno' the edge to be named as tour skipper, despite his lack of captaincy experience; he'd never done the job for England, although he had been deputising for Dean Richards as club captain at Leicester since the start of 1997.

As we all know, this tactic worked. 'Johnno' led the Lions from the front and set an example to everyone, getting the team in the right frame of mind to beat the Springboks. He rose to the huge challenge with aplomb, and although he captained in a different style from my own, leaving the tactical decisions on the field to those around him, he proved himself as a first-class leader. He was at the centre of everything the team did in South Africa, and was always ready to meet the Springboks head-to-head, a 'Tiger' both physically and mentally.

As a player he has always been completely committed and, in technical terms, he is world class in both the lineout and everywhere else around the field. On the Lions tour he further enhanced his international reputation. His tackling in South Africa was superb, and his general defensive work, rucking, mauling and distribution were just as good. He is a phenomenal athlete for such a big guy, and he commands the utmost respect from his teammates. But perhaps his biggest achievement in South Africa was to use these personal assets to help bond the diverse team together and to unite it behind him, sustaining the camaraderie through the demanding two-month, 13-game tour. It was never an easy task despite the early tour victories which set the team on the right road, and for this alone he deserves immense credit.

Martin may, at times, have found it somewhat uncomfortable standing up in front of the media before and after games, and even, perhaps, in the team meetings, because he's a broody and introverted giant. But these sorts of things always take some getting used to, and he seemed to carry them off well. Make no mistake, all of his England teammates were right behind him – those who were on the Lions tour, and those who had been left behind.

Despite the obvious choice of Martin as captain, I was surprised by some of the names included in the initial party but then excluded from the final 35. I think Catty's omission was the biggest surprise of all, because he'd been on fire in the second half of the domestic season. He carried on that great work for England in Argentina, and I was really pleased that he was eventually drafted into the Lions squad, and that he played – and played well – in the final Test at Ellis Park. The South Africans must have been glad that he wasn't on the tour from the start, because he could have made those first two Test defeats even more uncomfortable for the 'Boks.

There were one or two other marginal decisions which could have gone either way. The selectors picked Nick Beal as a wing – an interesting move, as he didn't really play in the position last season. And scrum-half Matt Dawson must have considered himself very lucky to have been selected ahead of Kyran Bracken and Andy Gomarsall, as he had been injured for much of the 1996–97 season. I know Kyran was gutted; he must have been packing his bags in readiness for the trip. But all credit to Matt, who took his chance and ended up as one of the try-scoring stars of the Lions tour.

After having provided four players on the 1993 Lions tour to New Zealand, the Bath contingent were initially very disappointed with our showing in the squad, with only Jerry Guscott a first choice for the tour. However, the subsequent addition of Mike Catt and Nigel Redman to the party was a real bonus for the club and, of course, for the two individuals. For 'Ollie' Redman it was the perfect way to cap a wonderful playing career.

Despite my personal disappointment, and that of some of my teammates, Fran Cotton still managed to assemble one hell of a physical and powerful Lions squad. They had to be, because it must have been a very gruelling tour, and a massive test of stamina as well as character. When the English Lions arrived in Australia for the one-off Test against the Wallabies soon after the tour had ended, it was clear that the contest was going to be one match too many after their efforts in South Africa. The boys had given their all and they needed a rest. It was hard enough for the England side which had played in Argentina to pick themselves up again after a month off. In contrast, the Lions came straight from Johannesburg, happy and victorious but nevertheless exhausted.

I'm still disappointed that I was left out of the squad. But I have always looked on selection for the 'next team up' in the playing hierarchy as a bonus: when I was playing as a student, the games I played for Durham County and England Students were something special, a reward for my skill and hard work. From then on it has been the same, culminating in my appointment as the England captain – the ultimate dream of any English rugby player. Bearing that in mind, it would have been churlish to have made too much of a fuss about my omission from the Lions squad. I am thrilled to have gone further than most other players in fulfilling my dreams and ambitions, and I hope that I haven't finished yet!

CHAPTER NINE

From the Sublime to the Ridiculous: Bath 1996–97

Wasps may have been crowned the Courage One champions in 1997, but there's a sting in the tail in store for the boys from London. Enjoy it while you can, because Bath will be back with a vengeance next season!

Despite finishing runners-up in the league, we were not at our best in 1996–97. From time to time we did get it right and play sublime rugby, and on occasions we absolutely slaughtered the opposition. We ran in a hatful of tries against Bristol, Leicester (at the back end of the season, at least), Harlequins, Orrell and Sale, to name but a few. But all too often we failed to deliver the killer blow to finish off some of our weaker rivals. We slipped up at crucial moments and were defeated six times in the league, sometimes losing our way in tight games which we should have won, conceding both the victory and the points. Losing tight matches – 11–5 to Sale and 9–6 to Northampton – was a new and unpleasant experience for the Bath team in the league, and it's one we don't intend to make a habit.

It was a traumatic and unsettled season in which there was disruption at every turn, until we suddenly ran into form in the last month or so of the campaign. From that point on we were terrific, but it was too late to make a difference in the league and cup competitions and to carry us to honours, so the trophy room is empty. Hopefully that will be put right in 1997–98.

Our season had begun badly. Contract negotiations for the new era of professionalism dragged on through the summer of 1996 and disrupted much of the important pre-season training schedule. We had so many problems with these negotiations during July that we didn't really start training properly until August. By then we were already well behind in terms of what we needed to have achieved to get off on the right footing.

What followed was also unsettling for the close-knit Bath family. The club management signed up a number of new, high-profile stars: not home-grown players from the domestic union code, but foreign stars from distant shores, some of them non-English speakers. We also snapped up two giants from the world of rugby league. Federico Méndez, German Llanes, Dan Lyle, Jason Robinson and Henry Paul all arrived in Bath with a mission to prove themselves in English club rugby union, and it generally wasn't as smooth and easy a transition as we might have expected.

Of course, other teams will argue that their new signings made the difference, turning them into serious League Championship contenders after having bordered on the mediocre in days gone by. That was true enough, and in some cases sides splashed out huge amounts for world-beating international playmakers and kickers. In the end it was a major factor in why we didn't win the League last season; games which were previously home bankers often became tense, close affairs thanks to these star names.

The game had clearly moved on in leaps and bounds during the close season and players and supporters had to come to terms with the new world of rugby. Although John Hall encouraged us to set out in pursuit of all the available domestic and European club honours we could muster in the 1996–97 season, having won the League and Cup double the year before, the fact of the matter was that we were never likely to maintain the total dominance of the domestic game that we had achieved for much of the last decade.

Professionalism – and money – have changed the face of rugby and now other teams have caught up with high-flying Bath. Today they all have the professional match-winning attitude to the game that we had adopted even as amateurs. The gaps have closed between the top clubs. Teams like Wasps, Harlequins and Saracens have dug deep and invested in skilful new players, and they are much stronger than they ever were before. Saracens practically had a new team for

1996–97. So, there are no easy games any more, and there are, perhaps, three or four further sides capable of causing an upset. Our stop-start season wasn't simply a question of Bath being less deadly. Something similar has happened in rugby league, where Wigan – so long the front-running and cup-winning, dominant force – have been caught in their stride. Bath too have been caught, having previously been well ahead in the race for honours.

Having said that, however, we did not play well for long periods of the season, and we played some terrible games. We were inconsistent, and it did take a long time for our hugely talented imports to get to grips with the English game and find the confidence to dominate their opponents – something which was ultimately worth waiting for. In the past we would somehow have got away with those really poor performances, and we would have inevitably scraped a victory by overwhelming the opposition with our power and our pride. But not any more. Our opponents have become too strong and too powerful to roll over without a real fight.

In addition, there were things going on behind the scenes which unsettled our preparations and our team spirit. There were major off-the-field developments at the Rec. We were deprived of the services of our long-term coach Brian Ashton, and then our friend, teammate and director of rugby, John Hall, was sacked – at roughly the same time as he had a date in the diary to take the dock in a well-publicised court case. Set these complex changes in the context of amateur rugby players coming to terms with a new professional lifestyle, and it doesn't necessarily add up to attractive, integrated, flowing rugby week in, week out. For Bath it most definitely didn't until late on in the season, when our game suddenly clicked. Everything that had gone before in the topsy-turvy world of professionalism fell into place and we began playing like a dream, having rediscovered our rhythm, style and hunger for victory. Then, even the very best could not live with the Bath onslaught.

If there was one turning-point that set us back on the right road it was our mauling of the Tigers at the Rec in mid-April, a game we won 47–9 and the highlight of our disappointing club season. In a blinding second-half display we wiped out Leicester's final hope of overturning Wasps' five-point lead at the head of Courage League One, and at the same time strengthened our hold on a Heineken Cup place. It was a tight start to the match, and we only led 14–9 at half-time. But, after the break, Bath were superb and we ran the Leicester team ragged, leaving them devastated, exhausted and battle worn from a gruelling season.

When the shackles came off we were a different team. We have so much talent in the squad at our disposal, but sometimes it's difficult to find the confidence to go out and perform at the top of your game. In the second half against Leicester, though, we found that missing spark, and all hell broke loose. It was a watershed performance, and critical for us in the longer term. Even though competition has always been very close between Bath and Leicester, psychologically the Tigers have had the edge for the last season or so, despite the fact that we really should have beaten them in the fixture at Welford Road. This home victory served as a timely reminder of the awesome ability of the Bath team, and the confidence flowed back for our remaining games, where we demolished Orrell, Sale and Gloucester.

The Bath crowd were magnificent during the game, and the lads not a little euphoric afterwards. We did feel a little sorry (and I stress a *little* sorry) for the Leicester side, after they had promised so much in all competitions and stumbled as the season wore on. At least they just made it back into Europe, now the biggest prize of all, courtesy of a last-minute equaliser in a nail-biting 20–20 draw with Sale. And, of course, they won – or should I say borrowed – the Cup.

Andy Robinson said after our victory against them that it takes special people to cope with the demands of league and cup rugby plus international competition, and the qualities are mental as well as physical. Leicester struggled at this crucial hurdle where, in times gone by, Bath have taken it in their stride. They did look tired, and the team was depleted by a few injuries, but let that take nothing away from our top-class performance in the last half-hour. Catty showed magnificent vision, spraying long, accurate passes and mixing the play, and Ade looked strong, fast and elegant in scoring twice. Our two Argentinian forwards Federico Méndez and German Llanes came into their own during the Tigers game. They played increasingly well as the season progressed, and they looked more menacing as the ground got harder and faster. Both of them are outstanding broken-field runners. Our American number eight Dan Lyle was also outstanding: big in the lineout, strong in the tackle and always the winner of 50-50 ruck and maul situations. He scored a great try, following a move he started from the lineout. It was a terrific afternoon in the sun.

Among one or two others, German and Dan took quite a while to settle into the Bath side, and that must have had an impact on our game in the early part of the season. When German arrived at the club he was selected to play for the seconds rather than the first team, which is both a humbling experience and a tough learning ground. German spent six or seven weeks grafting, and he had to fight his way into the firsts. Now he has settled down, and there is nothing being taken for granted. During the season German's English also significantly improved and, gradually, he began to smile and share a joke with the other players. As a result, he 'came out of his shell', and it showed on the pitch where he became much more dominant.

Dan is a phenomenal athlete, but he could be careless at times when he first arrived at the Rec. Occasionally he would try and pull off fancy one-arm reverse loop passes behind his back once he'd beaten three people, and lose the ball on the way. That's a thing of the past, and he really came on and learned about the English game. Dan has settled and that too showed in some great performances on the pitch.

But it wasn't just German and Dan 'settling down' which led to that big win against Leicester. It was the combination of a number of factors falling into place as if they were the final pieces of a difficult jigsaw. Perhaps most important of all was that the still relatively new Bath coaching duo of Andy Robinson and Clive Woodward was beginning to count. The man management at the club improved significantly as the season progressed, largely thanks to this partnership. Andy Robinson is already proving himself as a top chief coach and a first-class man manager, and he and Clive Woodward – along with Nigel Redman – make a great team. They trust each other and work well together. It's a blessing and promises to set us in good store for the new 1997–98 season, for which there are high expectations, particularly with the addition of Kiwi fitness guru Jim Blair. Jim is coming from Auckland in June to help us work with our fitness over the summer. He's a hard man, and his programmes are reputedly very tough, so we'll be fit for the new campaign. We already know that we have to be fitter than we were last season to play the game at its best. The players are ready for it, and they *really* want somebody to work them. And we know that it's going to be hard.

You could never find a more committed player than Andy Robinson ('Robbo'), and he gives the same total commitment to coaching as he has always given to playing. He was talking about 'retiring' last season, but we convinced him to play on a while longer; we still needed his massive presence on the pitch. Our game is based around having an open-side flanker who can get into the nooks and crannies on the field where the ball is hiding, but I knew that Robbo was torn between wanting to cut away from the playing so that he could give his full commitment to coaching. Robbo sensed that he could not be fully committed to his coaching role when he generally found his head at the bottom of a maul during training – a fair point! But we'll miss him when he stops playing. He is an integral part of what Bath rugby is all about.

As chief coach, Robbo chose Clive Woodward as his number two, and Clive's influence has already been profound. After leaving London Irish in November 1996 because of 'work commitments', Clive backtracked somewhat and soon began talking to Bath. He opened up negotiations with the club over Christmas 1996, well before John Hall left, and joined us before he was sacked. There was no underhand 'shuffling of the pack', although there were still questions asked in the press about the timing of Clive's appointment.

As a tracksuited coach rather than a suited manager, Clive has settled in very well. I didn't really know him before he came down, but I'm glad he made the move. He's a very strong character and wants to do things a certain way, but that's the right approach for the professional era. Clive is a businessman who has worked in a professional environment all his life, and he is now bringing that experience to Bath. As an 'outsider' he also brings us a different, fresh, and valuable new perspective.

Clive immediately took us back to basics in terms of skill training and drills, something that had been seriously lacking earlier in the season. Initially some of the players were a bit baffled, but we soon started to see the benefits. Now we need to keep on working hard and hopefully our skill levels will continue to improve in time for the new campaign.

When Clive arrived at the club, he saw our anguish. The club was in turmoil off the field and we weren't firing on it. He started just after Leicester beat us in the Pilkington Cup, easily the lowest point of our club season. The memory is still painful when I think about it. We selected the wrong side on the day, and our back row was very exposed. Robbo was not playing, and the balance was askew. It was one of Dan Lyle's first games for the team, and he played at open-side for half the time, and Eric Peters for the rest. But it didn't work and it showed. Our defence also played poorly, and we missed more tackles in that one fixture than I can remember us missing in all of our later games put together. After that awful defeat we had to go back to the drawing board to put our defence in order.

Clive also saw us struggle in the frustrating 11–5 defeat against Sale which summed up much of our campaign. It was already 11–5 at half-time, and despite the fact that we spent the whole of the second half on the attack and camped on their line, we couldn't finish the game off. All we needed was one score but we couldn't get it. We had chances galore, but it made no difference. We even managed to mess it up and drop the ball during an attack in the last minute, when it seemed easier to score. Our forwards were hammering all over their line, and we moved the ball in the backs and made an overlap. JC came haring into the line, just outside of yours truly, and I sensed that he was through the gap. I popped the ball up to him but it was very flat, and he dropped it. If my pass had been more accurate he would have scored. In one awful moment, it showed how small the difference is between winning and losing, how tiny the margin of error is between imperfection and perfection, and how one little instance in an 80-minute game can even make the difference between winning and losing a championship. You soon come to realise how those little things count, and how they all add up over the course of a season.

One of the problems last season was probably a lack of mental toughness. There was a distinct lack of confidence, and we were not playing the game as we should have been. The season felt like it was going from bad to worse. It was therefore no fun at all to be in the dressing-room after that Sale game, nor on the coach back to Bath. Defeat finally left our title defence in tatters, and we were left having to work really hard to ensure that we made it back to the money-spinning Heineken Cup.

Clive Woodward made a dramatic impact with a 'man-to-man' talk in the dressing-room after that game which put us back on the rails. He told us that our performance was not good enough. In fact, he said it was rubbish! 'I'd rather play well and lose 34–32 than lose 11–5 like that,' he said. 'You're not playing the game like it's meant to be played. It's got to be fun to watch and to play. Let's cut loose!' And that's what happened in the later games, against Wasps and Leicester to name but two. Clive Woodward made a big difference to the club, without doubt helping to fill the void left by Brian Ashton's departure.

When Brian walked out he left a huge hole behind, and there was a great deal of uncertainty about what was going to happen next. I was surprised when it happened. Technically Brian's a fantastic, gifted coach, and I got on with him very well at Bath. I had done so ever since I joined the club. He has a wicked sense of humour, but rarely smiles. Nigel Redman reckons that you only use 24 muscles in your face when you smile, and 50 when you frown. If it's true, Brian must have had the fittest face in the First Division!

However, although we got on, and still do, even I appreciated that Brian was not the right man to head Bath Rugby Football Club on the playing side, which was part of his grand plan. He wanted more authority, and more autonomy, without the responsibility that comes with it. He didn't want to take the difficult decisions, and he wasn't cut out to be a strong man manager.

There were a number of factors building up during the 1996–97 season which must have upset Brian and convinced him that it was time to leave. He didn't have a proper office, or a decent working environment. I don't think that he had been consulted about the new players being targeted to join the club for the 1997–98 season, or, conversely, which ones we might loan out. As head coach he got the hump, and rightly so. He probably felt a bit isolated. John Hall had to take some of the responsibility for that; he was not a great communicator. However, I don't think that there was any malicious intent whatsoever. John just never thought about discussing things with Brian.

There were also some outstanding contractual issues which needed to be sorted out between the club and Brian, and so the tension was beginning to rise on all counts. John then got into some trouble on the Saturday night after the first Harlequins game and he was 'out of the office' for the next few days, just when he was supposed to be meeting with Brian to settle some of these pressing issues. It was bad timing all round. Brian must have felt like saying 'Stuff you!'. But he should not have left the club in trouble by walking out with only one day's notice. It was hardly the honourable thing to do – although it was something that Brian had evidently done before, having also 'resigned' when Jack Rowell was in charge. From a managerial point of view, I don't think it was very easy to work alongside my friend Mr Ashton!

As soon as Brian walked out of the Rec, he came to meet me at home to discuss the predicament. We tried to sort things out, and I hoped we could persuade him to stay. Tony Swift, Ged Roddy and myself put together a new job description, one which fundamentally changed the balance between the director of rugby – Hally – and Brian as the head of coaching. We tried to accommodate some of Brian's demands, and I thought that we had virtually reached a compromise. Indeed, we conceded a fair bit of ground so that Brian could increase his role in the direction he was looking for. But when we went back to him with the offer, he still refused. Brian really was leaving.

By that time there was more to it, of course, and the Ireland job beckoned. Although we were not sure, we assumed that he must have another job on offer. Otherwise, I figure, he would have taken the Bath offer because it was practically giving him what he was looking for, in terms of both job responsibility and the role itself. Sure enough, we then found out that he had been officially appointed as the new Ireland coach. I think there had been a number of other offers made to Brian, including one from Cardiff. We certainly didn't think he would be going to join the England coaching set-up, although there were some confusing messages coming back from Jack Rowell. Although Brian obviously knew Jack better than anyone, probably personally as well as professionally, and had worked supremely well with him at Bath, it would have been difficult for Brian to go and work in an England coaching role because it would have meant that Jack would have needed to part company with Les Cusworth. That's why I felt it was a little strange when Jack told some radio reporters that he had tried to call Brian after he had walked out on Bath (although Brian told me that he never received a call from Jack!). It must have given Les an uneasy feeling. Perhaps Jack was playing his usual complex mind games.

However, I must admit that I was surprised when Brian took the job as Irish coach. He's over 50 already, and he had been talking to me about just four more 'rugby years' before retirement. He also lives in the South-west of England, not Ireland, and I know how much he likes it down there, so his travel arrangements will be interesting. But good luck to him; everyone wishes him well.

Immediately after Brian left the club scene, Robbo took command of coaching together with Nigel Redman, and Jon Callard helped to fill in the gaps. They all did magnificently well. We are very lucky to have experienced players like these in the team, and they proved themselves as good rugby coaches in their own right.

The Bath players have usually been able to sort themselves out and motivate each other in the past, regardless of what has been happening or not happening at management level. But even that motivation and drive was disrupted last season because we felt that the changes were having a direct impact on us, affecting our playing management.

It was therefore a very unsettling period, made more so by the many players turning their backs on conventional full-time employment to become rugby pros. Self-discipline suddenly became an even more important part of the game, because the new regime meant that you had time on your hands. A few players managed to keep their part-time or full-time jobs, and they may have found the changeover easier than my teammates who had got nothing outside their rugby. Those who have gone from full-time jobs and senior rugby to seven-day professional rugby are probably staring down a void in their lives. And with so little full-time player management and back-up for the first half of the season, it made the changeover even more painful.

During that period we only really had John Hall full time, and he was frantically trying to sort out the growing day-to-day demands of the club's administration. He had moved right away from the players. Even our fitness trainer Ged Roddy was part-time; his top priority was, and always had been, sport at Bath University. As the weeks passed we desperately needed more full-time staff − a dedicated administrator and a physio, for a start. It was all being addressed, but very slowly.

The introduction of two top imports from the game of rugby league had given all the Bath players a lesson in how to approach the professional era. Jason Robinson and Henry Paul may have been tired after their demanding exploits in the league code, but they always managed to give 100 per cent, in training as well as during games, and they were always smart and on time. Their businesslike approach was superb. They behaved like consummate professionals, and turned out to be really good club men. It must have been very difficult for Jason and Henry, coming straight from a rugby league season into a union season, and then going back without a break. But they must have known it was going to be pretty tough. I don't think they came for a rest! Even Jason and Henry, superstars of rugby league, had their problems adapting to the demands of rugby union. It was not the plain sailing that some had expected it to be, and it proved, once again, that the games are very different indeed.

We played the two cross-code fixtures against Wigan at the end of the 1995–96 season and, as well as being financial money-spinners for the club, we looked forward to the encounters – albeit with some trepidation. The games were good for us. Firstly we knew that we were going to get thumped by Wigan in the game played under rugby league rules, and we were: 82–6. Playing just four days after a sapping Pilkington Cup final victory against Leicester wasn't ideal, but we managed to put up a creditable performance, particularly in the second half when we dug deep, sorted out the organisational side of things and tackled like demons. The remarkable Martin Offiah, who began his career with the same club as my father, Rosslyn Park, returned from injury to run in six of Wigan's 16 tries in front of a crowd of 20,148 at Maine Road in Manchester. That in itself was a new and humbling experience for men wearing a Bath shirt. It would be fair to say that many of the players were scared before the game, yet they still went out and did the business – because the Bath team has real pride. Wigan were hard to stop and their lines of running were excellent, particularly those of the pack. They came on at pace. But, even so, I reckon that if we had had a few more practice sessions we might have kept the Wigan score down to 50 points rather than 80!

We then got our own back and rolled them over 44–19 in the game played under union rules at Twickenham in front of 40,000 people some two weeks later. That was despite one or two Wigan supporters backing an upset, and it totally vindicated our dominance of the rugby union code. Honour was therefore shared, and respect was mutual between the players, the fans and the administrators. I really enjoyed the two games, and it was good to experience the new disciplines of rugby league.

Despite the comments from then RFU secretary Tony Hallett, who said that it would be 'difficult for the two games not to merge' in the future, and RFL chief executive Maurice Lindsay, who added that there 'will be a unified game in five years', I reckon that if the two cross-code games proved anything, it was that the codes are still at a tangent in terms of style, approach, training and playing. Even the training regimes are completely different. In rugby league there is no contact during training. They seem to do a lot of weight training and explosive speed work. On the other hand, at Bath we do a lot of contact work, particularly – and not surprisingly – among the forwards. They don't get to look like that just by getting their heads down on a Saturday afternoon!

Both Jason Robinson and Henry Paul have great sporting and athletic talents. We all saw their supreme running skills at the Rec, and there is no question that the rugby league players were miles better in one-on-one situations. They have learned how to beat an opponent one-to-one from their code, whereas most union players have been taught to beat their man with a pass. In the league game you are encouraged to go one-on-one and take the man on, because it doesn't matter so much if you get caught – the ball is simply recycled. In contrast, in the game of rugby union you don't want to get caught, and you need to try and keep the ball alive.

Perhaps we hoped for too much too quickly when we initially started out on this experiment. Some pundits didn't even think it was an experiment, fully expecting the league boys to come in and dominate the game. Perhaps unsurprisingly, it didn't all go to plan and we put too many of our eggs in this one basket. In the end, we found that combining the two 'approaches' and the various skills of rugby league and rugby union had mixed results at Bath.

When Jason and Henry first came together at the Rec, they played in the match against Swansea. They were outstanding, and helped us notch up more than 80 points. As strong, dynamic runners, both of them were awesome on that occasion. But, on reflection, we should have realised that they had been given enough time and space to play to their strengths, meaning that they were able to play the ball flat and really show off their running skills. They played so well that we were lulled into a false sense of security. In reality both of them took a little bit longer to settle in after that honeymoon period, especially when it came to closer, tightly fought matches where the time and space were less evident.

Jason was probably the more successful of the two on balance. He is an absolutely electric runner. But once people knew that he was going to run rather than kick, he began to find it more difficult. In any game you've got to keep your opponent guessing. As soon as the other side knew Jason was going to run, they were all up in the line and hammering him, and it invariably put us under unneccessary pressure.

Our Bath management got carried away, and it did not take long for us to pay the price. After the superb Swansea game we made the mistake of going over the top. Henry and Jason were considered 'the bee's knees' and the answer to all of our prayers; they had to be picked. It resulted in us making one particularly serious mistake, when we did not pick Jon Callard for the game against Cardiff. In that Heineken Cup match we put Henry on the wing and Jason at full-back, and played without our recognised goal-kicker. Instead Catty took over the kicking duties, and he had an off-day which cost us dearly. We should have beaten Cardiff, having outplayed them completely. We hadn't dominated a side like that and been beaten for some time. They only broke into our half three times in the first half, and they were awarded three penalties.

That big European game against Cardiff was the beginning of our mixed fortunes with the two rugby league players. I think that we perhaps foolishly laid it all at their feet, following our hearts rather than our heads, so much so that we disrupted our existing team's 'family spirit'. We sometimes unbalanced the side so that we could accommodate their talents. Although Henry, and Jason in particular, were massive influences early on in the season, they went back to their rugby league careers at Christmas, and I think that this also somehow upset the chemistry of the tight-knit Bath club. It's very difficult to achieve but you need to strive for a settled squad, and if changes are going to be made, it's better if new players are brought into the frame in time for summer training, and then stay with the team throughout the season. It helps with the bonding process. There will always need to be some mid-term flexibility, but this would be the most ideal arrangement. Furthermore, when

Henry and Jason left halfway through the season, it left us without cover in some key positions.

As a result, I doubt that we will use league players again. That's up to the club, but I think it would be unlikely. It certainly proved much harder for league players to make the crossover than anybody might have expected, even though it sometimes paid handsome dividends. I will always remember the fantastic game Jason played against Bristol. But this rollercoaster ride between success and failure was really the story of our season.

The Heineken Cup was something that we had looked forward to for a long time, and our quarter-final appearance has whetted our appetite. This pan-European Cup is our prime target for the 1997–98 season. I'm looking forward to the competition, and I welcome its expansion.

As well as the match against Cardiff, we also played Edinburgh, Pontypridd, Treviso and Dax, and the last two, in particular, were really hard games. The Treviso encounter taught us new tricks, with the Italians approaching the game slightly differently from the English. They played it very well, and certainly gave us something to think about. Treviso posed questions of the Bath team that we had never had to answer before. They protected their own ball very well, and dived in over the top to shield it. It made it hard to get the ball back once it was in their possession. They were also very fit, and played the game at pace – almost in the 'Bath style'! Treviso moved the ball around really well, and kept it alive as we do. It made for an interesting and challenging match. There is no doubt that the Italian nation is now a force to be reckoned with in world rugby, at both club and international level.

Despite our good performance against the Italians, however, I don't think that we would have beaten Brive in a semi-final on French soil. Like Cardiff I think we would have found it very hard over there, but that's all part of the magic of this exciting new competition. Playing the European Cup match against Cardiff was the closest thing to playing an international that I have experienced at club level. There was a great atmosphere. It was a step up, and even though we lost, this is the level at which the game must be played in the future so that we can compete with the southern hemisphere sides, who are more used to regular top-flight rugby.

By the time we had been defeated away from home at Harlequins in the Courage League, we felt that we had lost our way more than once too often, and the defence of our League title looked in some peril. The game against the Quins took place at the Stoop in mid-January, and it was already the third game we had lost that we should have won. There were other horror afternoons such as the games against Leicester and Wasps at the Rec, where we had all the possession and chances galore, but failed time and time again to make the possession count in our favour.

Harlequins have played far, far better than they did in that game against us, and still lost. All that we needed was one score and I think they would have cracked, but that score just didn't come. As well as creating enough chances to win the game, we also had a few refereeing decisions go against us. These sorts of things can and do cost championships.

Afterwards we were particularly despondent because we knew it was a game we should have won. We are not used to losing, and we are not good at coping with defeat. Yet you can't turn up and *expect* to win games now; it simply doesn't happen. You have got to be 'balls-out' all of the time, all 15 players and the subs, because even teams outside the top four can turn you over quite easily if you're not on top of your game. But it was not worth anyone giving us a dressing-room rollocking on this occasion, because we didn't lose through laziness or a lack of effort. We would have deserved a ticking-off if we hadn't tried hard enough. It was just bad finishing, and that made it worse.

However, as Leicester also lost in that round of games, the Bath team still felt that there was plenty to play for with half the season left, even though we knew we were not playing consistently well. It's here that Robbo had an influence. He always likes to accentuate the positive, and has a great attitude. If there was anyone who could help bring the enthusiasm back to our game, it was him.

During the 1996–97 season there was only one game where we were well and truly beaten, and that was against Northampton. We were stuffed, albeit 9–6. It was similar to the game against Sale, where we had a lot of the ball and couldn't score. However, all credit to Northampton on that occasion. They tackled very well, and deserved to win. We lost fair and square, and it was quite a shock to the Bath contingent.

The 25–25 draw with Wasps at Loftus Road in early April was another of the games we should have won. Despite everything, a victory would have put us right back on the heels of the league leaders and made the run-in very uncomfortable for the Londoners.

We started off as if our lives depended on the victory, and thanks to some quick and cunning thinking from Catty on the stroke of half-time we went in 13–6 ahead. We won a penalty for offside in front of the posts and Mike strolled to the mark without indicating the kick at goal. The Wasps defence stood dreaming while he tapped the ball and broke on the blind side to give Jerry a run over the line. We increased our lead in the second half when Ade scored, and then Jerry ran in a debatable try (was the ball in touch?). At that point we felt that we were home and dry, but we threw away the points. Alex King stole through to score a try, and then the ever-reliable Gareth Rees equalised with a conversion at the death. Once again we travelled home dreadfully disappointed. It was one of a number of long and silent journeys back to Bath!

It was in stark contrast with some of Bath's free-scoring performances, like the 84–7 victory against Sale later on that month. This match was notable for being a 12-try record-breaking league win, with Catty and Jerry Guscott in inspirational form, and Dan Lyle barnstorming in the teeming rain. But it also told us more about what could happen next season, when the fixture congestion will be worse than ever thanks to the heavy demands being placed upon top sides by the new Allied Dunbar Premiership, the 'Pilkington Cup' (which will have a new sponsor next season), the enhanced 'home and away' European Cup plus internationals. Sale had to field what was effectively their second team for this game, because of a fixture pile-up of seven matches in just 24 days. Despite the score it made for an unsatisfactory evening's sport, and highlighted something that is even more likely to happen in the 1997–98 season – particularly if we do well in both cup competitions and the weather intervenes to postpone a few games. It could cause chaos. If there was any evidence required in support of an urgent restructuring of the club season, this game was it. Robbo may be on to something when he argues that in the short term we should try to play two midweek matches in September this year, when the grounds are in peak condition, and a Christmas league fixture to attract the seasonal crowds. But what we really need is fewer games!

The summer of 1997 will be an important period of consolidation for Bath RFC. The arrival of fitness coach Jim Blair will make a difference, and without the contractual problems which dogged our pre-season last year, we should be able to manoeuvre our way through the build-up as planned. There should be a lot more continuity this year too, and we should be helped by the fact that we will probably be providing fewer players for international duty. In the past Bath have been placed under heavy pressure by having to release so many players for internationals. Now other clubs are having to learn to cope with those added selection pressures, not least Leicester.

We'll be signing a few new players, and have already put out offers. Mark Regan and Russell Earnshaw have already joined us, and I am sure there are one or two more in the pipeline. Hopefully we will all have got to grips with professionalism. I don't think that our general rugby union culture is as hardworking as it should be in terms of how much we train. I suppose I have been as guilty as anyone in this respect, because I still have other things to do, such as my Druid job. As things didn't go so well for us in 1996–97, I think it will give us just the spur we need to be really critical of ourselves over the break, and come back hungrier than we have ever been for a new season. Luckily we are all there to support each other, and the Bath rugby 'family' will pull through.

I'm sure that you couldn't find a closer group of friends than the guys at Bath RFC, because everyone has been through so much together. Obviously you are closer to some players than you are to others, but I have so many good mates at the club that it's not overdoing it to call it a 'family'. It has always been a close-knit environment because most of us live in or around the city, and we spend a lot of time at the club and in the clubhouse. With the advent of professionalism we are seeing more and more of each other, so we've got to get on! There were times last season when we felt as if we had been on tour, and on some occasions we had been. During one busy spell we were up in West Hartlepool for three days and in Sale for two, and back training in Bath in between. Under these circumstances there is no way you can avoid becoming close.

There's a good mix of characters at the club, and we are all from different backgrounds with different intellects and interests. But, without exception, everybody mucks in together. The wit is always razor sharp, and the dressing-room banter is unforgiving. There are no soft touches, and there is no room for the weak. I am sure it's the same in most senior rugby clubs. If you are going to make it to this level you have got to have something about you. Even so, when new players arrive at the club they get a good going-over, being tested mentally as well as physically. If they are not up to it they generally leave. That has been changing gradually, thanks to the advent of professionalism, but it remains a somewhat uncomfortable environment for outsiders. Without fail, everybody will give you stick. It doesn't matter at all if you have been successful elsewhere, like in the rugby league code or abroad – in fact, it probably makes it worse!

Looking around the players at the club makes for some interesting psychological and physiological profiling. For instance, take one of my close pals, John Mallett in the front row. He is a huge, domineering player, 6ft 1in and 16 stone, and one of the most aggressive players in the team. He also has one of the most massive heads in the game, and I, for one, would not like to be hit by him and his head! If John hadn't had one or two injuries he would be even closer to the full England squad, although he's pretty much there already. The changes at the club have probably benefited John.

I knew that he had been very unhappy with Hally because 'the director' had always favoured Victor Ubogu ahead of him. I also know that he was looking at moving to another club. Now Hally has left, I think and hope he's happy to stay. John is a great bloke, and Yolanda and I get on very well with him and his wife Emma. He also does a mean Barry White impression.

Victor, on the other hand, is an extraordinary character. Both Victor and Steve Ojomoh ('Ojo') are terribly lazy, but I reckon that if I had to choose between the two of them, Victor is probably the lazier. If he improved his fitness, he would be one of the most phenomenally explosive rugby players in the country. If he were fit, he would also be the best player in his position around, because of his immense power, footballing ability and his lineout play. But neither Victor nor Ojo works hard enough. These days Victor has got so many business interests that it's bound to affect his training regime.

He has, however, made us giggle over the years, and when he first joined the club he was a spoilt brat. I can remember one tantrum – and not the only one – when he refused to get on the team bus on tour in Australia because he thought that someone had nicked one of his cassette tapes. It was found under the bed in his room! Gradually he came to be more at home, and he's changed. He is nothing like as difficult as he once was, and he's become much more relaxed – indeed, sometimes a bit too relaxed.

There tends to be a lot of good banter between myself and Steve Ojomoh. In training we have occasional head-to-head sprint challenges, and there is inevitably a game on between us to prove who is the faster runner. He always thinks that he is quicker than me, but I always beat him! On the one occasion where we had a proper race I won, and then he had the astonishing cheek to tell a reporter from *The Times* that he'd been victorious. When it was published Ojo was in seventh heaven. There it was in black and white; he'd beaten me, the report said, so it must be true. So here and now I would like to correct that erroneous newspaper report, and put the record straight: I won that series, not Ojo!

Then there's hooker Graham Dawe (Richard Graham Reed

Dawe, or 'Dawesy'), for whom I have the utmost respect. He has been one of the core men in Bath's ongoing success over the last decade. Although he has a house near Bath and he often stays there, he has also travelled thousands of miles on the Bath RFC account during his time with the club, backwards and forwards between Bath and his farm at Milton Abbott on the Devon and Cornwall border. I used to live with my parents near where he comes from and it's a long, long drive to Bath and back. That's dedication and commitment for you. We have also started calling him 'HM', short for 'Hard Man'. He's always fighting and he can fly off the handle sometimes, but he has put everything he has into Bath Rugby Club and for that we all treasure him. HM is now a proud father, and perhaps his little girl will calm him down!

Federico Méndez is a wonderful and very skilful ball player, and he has a good sense of humour too. His English is just about good enough to understand what we are saying about him! I sometimes wonder whether he is as aggressive as we would like for a hooker, not being a player who is going to punch and kick. By that I am not insinuating that forwards have to have those specific 'qualities', but you do need people who are tough in the pack.

Kevin Yates is the original 'Mr Smiley', and you rarely see him without a big grin on his face. He likes to lark about, sometimes too much for his own good. Again he is another very strong runner with the ball, and very powerful. His partner Dave Hilton is the complete opposite, the quiet man in the team who just gets on with it. He gets his head down, and does the nitty-gritty.

Nigel 'Ollie' Redman is one of our long-time and almost legendary leading lights of the second row, a guy who has played in, and won, a remarkable nine John Player/Pilkington Cup finals. He and fellow lock Martin Haag are not dissimilar in many ways, although Haagie did not play for England until the 1997 Argentina tour, whereas Ollie has won around 20 caps. They are often unsung heroes, and both mean a lot to the club.

These two do a lot of hard work week in, week out, and they are both good ball handlers and runners. But time waits for no man, and Ollie's getting on. Like his close mate Andy Robinson, Ollie will be

33 when the new season gets under way, and these days his body seems to need putting back together after every game. It's getting to the point where I am not sure we can rebuild him. It's anybody's guess how long he is going to last, but he is on a massive high after his Lions success in South Africa.

In terms of winning a regular England slot, I suspect Martin will always suffer from not being quite tall enough to really compete with the big men at international level – despite being 6ft 5in! But he's a very physical player with a good heart, and he's Bath through and through. He is a top man in the club scene, and I, for one, have a lot of respect for him. Martin is always straight and to the point, but he does enjoy beating up the little men in training. He never seems to pick on the big blokes – I wonder why! Like Kevin Yates, he's a bit of a bully.

What can I say about Andy Robinson? He is a man of integrity, a phenomenal player and a great guy. Now he is stepping down from his role as open side for the club he is transferring all his enthusiasm and energy for the game, as well as his positive thinking, to the coaching side, and I would imagine that he will have a long-term coaching career with us at Bath. He has already proved himself as a top coach and a good man manager. In the late 1980s he was voted European Player of the Year, and he is also an ex-British Lion. He was somewhat unlucky not to have won more than his eight England caps.

Richard Webster and Nathan Thomas are both relatively new. Nathan is still a youngster but he has a lot of potential. Richard is another hard man, and he'll probably be working on JC's patio as I write, he's that sort of guy. He's also another of the jokers in the team. He is a particularly good addition to the squad, and it was a shame that he was injured for a lot of the 1996–97 season, along with Scottish number eight Eric Peters, who was also out for quite a while.

In the back division there are a lot of talented youngsters coming through, and they will keep the competition for places very tough. They may only be 18 and 19 years old but they're good, and they're going to get better. Matt Perry, Joe Ewens and John Pritchard are all pressing for places this coming season. These boys have come straight into professional rugby without ever having had regular employment outside the sport. It will therefore be very interesting to see how they cope with professionalism as a way of life. They are some of the first players coming through who will need to come to terms with these new demands, and I look forward to seeing how they do. They all have a lot of potential, but it's not just a question of ability nowadays, it's also how you cope with the demands of the professional game. Charlie Harrison is another of our skilful youngsters, and he is now 'coming out of his shell', having initially been very quiet.

Sadly, Scottish scrum-half Andy Nicol was injured for most of the 1996–97 season. Andy's an incredibly talented player and very committed, but he has been made to suffer with injury after injury and he has never really managed to get enough continuity in his game as a result. One way or another Bath have struggled at scrum-half in terms of continuity since Richard Hill left the club. It really has been a problem area for us. If Andy were fully fit it would have been a breeze but, because he has picked up regular injuries, we've had to chop and change between Charlie Harrison and Ian Sanders, and, more often than not, neither player has got it quite right. Andy will be Bath captain in the 1997–98 season and I wish him well; he will make a good captain.

Fly-half Richard Butland is a very underrated player. Last season he was picked ahead of Catty for a couple of games when Mike was having a bad spell and Richard was playing very, very well. But then Mike started firing on all cylinders and he had to go back to sitting in the wings. Richard is a real wind-up merchant. We call him 'Butt-face' as in the television cartoon 'Beavis and Butt-head', because he's always moaning and groaning. Butt-face is quite a character.

Mike Catt is one of my closest friends at the club. He and his girlfriend Debbie spent Christmas with our family a couple of years ago, and Yolanda and I have been on holiday with them a few times. We all get on very well. I know for a fact that Catty was offered a phenomenal amount to move to Richmond last year, but he didn't take it, and I think that that has somehow worked to his advantage, because he is getting better and better as a player wearing the Bath shirt. Ultimately I think he'll be a centre, which is his best position. What's more, I think that he'll play for England in this position at some stage. He switched to centre for Bath, outside Stuart Barnes and myself, when Jerry Guscott was injured a few seasons ago, and that was probably the best midfield season that we have ever had. Some of the tries we scored were quite superb. I particularly remember one we ran in against Bristol which was magnificent.

In the midfield, Jerry Guscott always has the potential to be an absolute genius. There is no doubt that, on his day, Jerry can do things that no other player can do. I have seen Jerry get himself out of tight corners nobody else could have, and his running ability is sublime. In terms of attacking options, he is the tops. But every now and then he does crazy things, and on odd occasions he just doesn't seem bothered. He can be so laid-back. I have got nothing but respect for Jerry as a player, but off the field he's incredibly selfish, and he knows it – although he has certainly mellowed in his old age, and, of late, has been known to show amazing generosity (mine's a pint, Jerry!).

Adedayo Adebayo ('Ade') is another laid-back character and one of the nicest guys around, but while he may be laid-back he is also very powerful, and deceptively fast. Again he picked up a few nagging injuries during the 1996–97 season, which upset his rhythm. Ade was playing very well at the start of the season, and he fully deserved his selection for the England team. But then he got injured, and any injury, however small, sets you back. I hope he'll be back to his quickest in the new campaign.

Wing Jon Sleightholme ('Sleights') had a mixed season. He didn't get the first-team opportunities to begin with because of Jason Robinson, but then he did pretty well for England in the Five Nations. Later on in the season he slipped back again and wasn't playing so well. Mentally, Sleights can blow hot and cold. He tends to drift in and out of games very easily, and at the end of last season he was drifting out of them rather more than into them! Off the field Sleights is another good pal, and Yolanda and I get on well with him and his wife Julie. He is always trying to take me shopping so that he can act as my fashion adviser and buy me some decent clothes. I think he'd love to see me wearing something other than a tracksuit. He'll be lucky!

Jon Callard ('JC') is probably my best mate at the club. He had his ups and downs at the club during the 1996–97 season, and I think that he felt the pressure at times, particularly in the second half of the season when his kicking – obviously an important part of his game – was not going very well. JC always works very hard in training, and he is another completely committed player. We are just so lucky to have men like him turning out for the team. When the referee's whistle blows he's a different person, much stronger and more aggressive on the pitch than he is off it. He gets himself so fired up that he will mouth off to anyone, – however big they are – and he is always liable to clout the biggest person he can find. In fact, he will invariably pick on somebody bigger than him in a confrontation. I think it's some kind of release more than anything else. JC and his wife Gail are close friends.

Socially, I see a lot of JC, Catty and John Mallett, and as you spend more and more time with them you gradually begin to notice the odd habit. I've had the chance to observe JC in some detail because we room together. There's nothing too horrific to relay, but, as a 'for instance', JC always puts plasters on his feet before a game and nobody really knows why! I think he had a verruca or something once upon a time, which he used to patch up during games, and it turned into a habit – despite the fact that there's now nothing wrong with his feet at all. He also makes the tea on matchday mornings; these days I'm banned from the tea-making because every time I made it last season we were beaten!

Everybody changes in the same place. Even when we go to play away games, we tend to change in the same position, which is very odd. I always change in the corner with Ollie Redman. Unlike some, I don't put my kit on in any particular order and I'm not superstitious, but I always wear a little pair of white Nike socks underneath my rugby socks. I don't know why. I just started doing it and it's something that I have carried on ever since.

When we run out on to the pitch I now have to run out at the front, but when I started playing for Bath I used to run out three from the back. Gareth Chilcott always made a point of running out at the very back and I think it was Richard Hill who ran out one before him, so I always ended up running out three from back. We are creatures of habit – and at Bath we like that habit to include winning. We'll be seeing to that next season.

CHAPTER TEN

Head to Head with the Pumas

I'm back at home in Bath after a month on tour in Argentina which was full of highs, a few lows and quite a few surprises. Perhaps the biggest surprise of all was that my Bath teammate Nigel 'Ollie' Redman was called away from our England tour to join the British Lions second row in South Africa. Having virtually pensioned the old chap off into a coaching role for Bath, it came as a shock to all of us – not least of all Nigel himself who, at 32, thought Jack Rowell was joking when he broke the news.

When Ollie got his last-minute England call-up for the Argentina tour as a replacement for the unlucky Gareth Archer, we thought it would put the final gloss on his tremendous playing career. That's why Andy Robinson took Ollie aside and suggested that, when he returned home, it would be the perfect opportunity for him to announce his retirement from both international and Bath club rugby. I think Ollie was a bit surprised that Robbo had asked him to hang up his club rugby boots. But as Ollie is famously accident-prone and injury-prone, and as he had recently gone through a knee operation, Robbo's suggestion was not cruel or unkind. So, with that in mind, who would have thought that three or four weeks later he'd be called up to play for the Lions, and then be named as captain for the tourists' midweek game against the Free State Cheetahs, a match which turned out to be a great victory for the British Isles and for the indestructible Ollie Redman. Rather than buckle under the physical pressure, Ollie rose to the immense challenge and relished the battle. He is what the Lions are all about. Robbo has already taken a lot of stick for his dodgy judgement, and for even thinking that Ollie was running low on gas! Mr Nigel

Redman will surely now come back from Africa on such a high that he'll play on for Bath for at least another year.

We heard about Ollie's call-up on the morning of our final team run-through before the second Test against the Pumas. Jack took Ollie and me aside and asked me who was going to play instead of Nigel now that he'd been called up for the Lions – and then he winked at me. I looked at Ollie and Ollie looked at me, and then he said, 'I can't believe it.' And Jack replied, 'Nor can I!'

Once Jack had explained that it really wasn't a bad joke, and we'd both picked ourselves up off the floor, Ollie was asked what he wanted to do about playing in the second and final Test against Argentina. Ollie said that he wanted to play, but if delaying was going to jeopardise his chances of playing for the Lions then he felt that he'd better leave for South Africa immediately. As it happened he had no choice, as the next available flight had already been booked by the Lions management. Even if he had not been able to get a flight immediately and had stayed that extra day or so, which would have enabled him to don his England jersey again, I don't think that Fran Cotton would have wanted him to play in the second Test. Fran would not have wanted to risk yet another injury.

It was much the same situation with Mike Catt, although Catty must have hoped he would be called up as a replacement for the Lions at some time during our Argentina tour. He played so well in the latter part of the season that he must have expected to go in the original tour party, and he would have been upset when his name was omitted. But Mike is such a versatile player that he was always likely to end up on a plane to South Africa whichever of the backs was injured, and with some excellent performances at fly-half on the Lions tour Mike has proved that he should have gone in the first place. In truth, we expected plenty of injuries, and we weren't wrong.

It certainly didn't take Catty long to pack his bags and dash off to the airport, on his way 'back home' to South Africa. When he first left Port Elizabeth for a short holiday in England, having played a handful of times for Eastern Province, he could not have imagined that one day he would be one of the England élite, returning to South Africa wearing the red shirt of the British Lions.

Mike's flight from Argentina had already been booked by the Lions management team, and he was on his way on the Monday before we really had the chance to assess the ramifications for our international head-to-head decider against the Pumas on the following Saturday. The England management were clearly unhappy that some of their key players were now being snatched from under their noses, and by the way in which it was being done. At least Catty and Ollie had had a taste of Argentina, however, and both gave their all in the memorable first Test which showed what talent we now have at our disposal in the English game.

Although the England side in Argentina was severely disrupted as a result of the parallel Lions tour, with 18 members of our usual squad hunting with the Lions, the team spirit came together quickly and remained first class throughout the tour which gave some of our talented young players the opportunity to gain deserved debut caps. It also gave one or two older hands the chance to re-establish their credentials with the main man, Jack Rowell.

All in all the tour was a huge step forward for the England set-up, both playing and administrative, and although we lost a couple of games, the trip put down a marker for English rugby. The world can now see how much our game has developed and flourished since the introduction of professionalism. It also gave perhaps the first clear indication that English rugby now has strength in depth and enough talented young players to make a real impact come the 1999 World Cup.

With all the media focus on the magnificent Lions success – which rammed home the news of the massive improvement in our domestic game – some pundits may have missed the significance of the England tour, the first with professional players – and my first overseas tour as an England captain.

It took us a good 22 hours to fly to Argentina via Madrid, and while we were upgraded on the longest leg of the arduous flight from Spain to Argentina, it still felt like a very, very long journey. It's strange, but I'd never appreciated that South America is quite so far away. The trip took three planes and four landings in all. Ever cost-conscious, we travelled Economy over to Madrid, wedging some of the taller and beefier players into their seats for the short journey to the Spanish capital! Jack Rowell quipped about the journey: 'I reckon Hannibal with his elephants got over the Alps quicker than we got to Argentina. And he didn't have to represent a national team!'

We had met and trained at Bisham Abbey on the weekend that we departed, and then arrived in Argentina at lunchtime on the Monday, with a game planned for the Wednesday. There was no time at all to get back into the swing of things after a three-month lay-off from international rugby, and with a very different-looking England squad *in situ*. But I think it was generally appreciated by everyone on the trip that there was no time for messing about as there was plenty to do to get the approach and attitude 'in the groove', ready for the hard and very imminent game against Argentinian provincial champions Cordoba.

With so many new England faces on the flight, and so much still up for grabs, all of the players quickly showed their professionalism and dedication by knuckling down to the gruelling task ahead. Their energies were soon entirely focused in the right direction, probably encouraged by the fact that, as we set out, there was no clear distinction between the international and midweek sides. Literally every position on the field was open to debate and, with prized international caps at stake, there was a real opportunity for virtually every player on the tour to make a name for himself and play a meaningful part. And many of them did. Thanks to sterling performances from some of the new boys, competition for places will be hotter than ever in the 1997–98 season.

We spent much of the tour based in Buenos Aires city centre, and, save an enjoyable trip to a winery and playing video games in a nearby arcade from time to time, we were training and playing virtually all the way. Luckily the facilities in Argentina were very good and the grounds were generally in great nick, which helped our preparations. The pitches were quite hard, and the playing surfaces were not unlike those at home in England during the autumn months, before the grounds get wet, soft and muddy. That was with one exception: the rock-hard pitch for the game against Cuyo in Mendoza between the two Tests.

I was worried about that first game against Cordoba at the Chateau Carreras stadium, and not just because they were bound to provide very stiff opposition for what was, in many ways, a scratch England side. The pack was bound to be under pressure coming to terms with the huge power and technique of the Argentinians' scrummaging. Furthermore, Cordoba had beaten the Italian tourists eight years before, and later on had caused some concern to both South Africa and France. This time round they named five internationals in their squad and were intent on causing an upset. But my main worry was that we hadn't had enough time to pull the side together. A lot of players like to get straight into the first game of a tour, but this confrontation came literally 48 hours after we had landed, giving us little or no time to acclimatise and shake the long flight from our systems.

One of the major problems with most rugby tours is that you tend to arrive a whole week or even ten days before the first game. That's too long to sit around waiting and preparing, getting tense and nervous, because you always want to get going. But a gap of just two days was too short. In future, we need to strike a balance between the two extremes, perhaps leaving a gap of four or five days clear.

It was therefore a terrific boost for all of the squad to go into the first game of a hard six-match tour, play well and win 38–21. With Paul Grayson already with the Lions in South Africa, Catty saw it as his golden chance to firmly establish himself as the first-choice England fly-half, and he was still brimming with confidence after his terrific performance in England's last Five Nations game of the season against Wales. He was also eager to put the memory of his last international performance against an Argentinian side – the match against the Pumas at Twickenham in December '96, his worst game for England – behind him and to prove a point to Fran Cotton. Catty had come back as a bigger and better player after he had been dropped following that pre-Christmas game, and, with the number ten shirt still up for grabs on this trip, his performance against the formidable Cordoba side left us in no doubt that he would be one of our key play-makers on the tour.

Two other players came back into the side and proved their worth. Kyran Bracken got the nod over Andy Gomarsall at scrum-half for this game and played a blinder, and Richmond skipper Ben Clarke was back leading the pack and grateful for another opportunity to prove his value. The fixture could have been a tricky one, but thanks to two smartly taken tries from Kyran, who played really well, 18 points from Catty and a try from lock Ollie Redman – making his first England appearance for three years – we emerged comfortable victors. Yours truly also got in on the scoring act with a try courtesy of one of our new boys, Wasps centre Nick Greenstock, but it was Catty's sizzling 50-metre solo effort that grabbed the headlines. He chipped the ball forward and sprinted to collect it on the full and run it in under the posts. It was a 'staggering effort', according to the manager. 'You will have to go a long way to see anything better,' said Jack.

Our confidence surged after the win in the cold Cordoba night air, and with the four new caps giving a very good account of themselves, not only was it a relief for us to have hit the ground running but it also gave us virtually the perfect start – except for one off-the-field incident. Chris Sheasby had his passport and some credit cards pinched from the team bus just before that Cordoba game. We'd been told not to leave valuables in our room, but we hadn't had time to put some of the bits in the hotel safe, so Chris put his valuables in a bag and brought it to training on the bus. He left the bag on the bus and it walked!

Our second fixture of the tour was on the following Saturday against Buenos Aires at the city's Cricket and Rugby Club, and we were narrowly beaten simply because our goal-kicking wasn't up to scratch. There was no disgrace in being beaten 23–21 by a side which contained 13 internationals, but had Alex King and then Mark Mapletoft slotted a few more goal-kicks in this game we would have been comfortable winners. In all we missed eight kicks, five penalties and three conversions. Although Alex missed all three of his conversion attempts and a penalty, 'Tofty' ended up as the main culprit. He missed four penalty attempts in the last eight minutes, and had he taken just one we would have sneaked a victory to keep our 100 per cent tour record intact. Alas, he missed all four, but even though one hit the post, he was big enough not to make any excuses. Goal-kicking wins matches, and you can't afford to miss chances at this level. That was proven to be the case as Buenos Aires kicker José Çilley slotted 18 points, from five penalties and a drop goal. I think both Alex and Mark learned a great deal from the mistakes made in that game.

However, we did score three tries, which provided some consolation, through Ben Clarke, Jim Mallinder and myself. And although we were defeated, I was beginning to feel increasingly confident about the way things were going, along with feeling in good shape personally. I finally felt that I was completely over my pre-Christmas injuries.

Seventy-two hours later we bounced back with a commanding 58–17 victory over Argentina 'A'. The win was doubly satisfying in that we only fielded two full international caps. Virtually all of the players who hadn't played in the Buenos Aires defeat got a game against Argentina 'A', and the side hared off to a great start, scoring three tries to go 24–0 up early on. We then showed a little inexperience, allowing the Argentinians to score three tries and pull the score back to 24–17 by the interval.

At that stage the Pumas must have felt that they were in with a shout of victory, and when Mark Mapletoft's kicking boots temporarily left him again during two penalty attempts either side of half-time, we did wonder whether there could be another defeat in store. We could not have been more wrong, and any talk of an Argentinian victory was forgotten soon after the break.

Haagie scored a precious debut England try, which settled us down again after the interval. It had exactly the desired effect in that it set us back on the road to victory and, not for the first time this season, we went on the rampage in the last 20 minutes to whip the shadow Pumas, scoring another 34 points without reply.

More than anyone, Gloucester's Mark Mapletoft answered his critics after a poor display in the previous game. He returned to the scene of Saturday's kicking crime and hit back, scoring 18 points from full-back – a position he hadn't played in for a couple of years. He told me that he was more nervous about playing at full-back than he was about taking the kicks, so he deserves special credit. I was particularly pleased for him and it gave us a valuable morale boost just days before the first Test. The tour was back on track with some style. We scored eight flowing tries, refused to get drawn into a dour forward battle, and played the game on our terms, moving the ball around with some panache to create plenty of openings. Two tries each from Jos Baxendell and David Rees, one each from Andy Gomarsall and Haagie, another superb chip-and-run try from Catty and a glorious debut England score from Harlequins wing Daren O'Leary left us very satisfied with our evening's work. It went so well that Kevin Yates, Tony Diprose and Haagie all played themselves into the reckoning for the first Test. Jack said that the standard of our play owed a lot to how the Courage League improved throughout the season. Watching the urgency, authority and maturity shown by some of our young players, he was clearly right.

The Bath contingent was feeling good and we all went out to supper to celebrate John Mallett's birthday on the Wednesday night after the game against Argentina 'A', a few days before the first Test. We had further cause to celebrate, following Martin Haag's call-up for his first full cap. The international team for the Test had been announced and Haagie had found out that he was included, so there was plenty of good news to cheer, and our Argentinian friends Freddie (Federico Méndez) and German (Llanes) joined us for dinner in Buenos Aires. Not surprisingly the banter was excellent, especially between Haagie and German who would face up to each other on the field soon afterwards. Martin was thrilled, and he knew he would be partnering his friend and Bath teammate Ollie Redman against the Pumas, which made it even better. Haagie has put so much into the game, and had been close on a number of occasions. He's consistent and very talented and we knew he'd give it 100 per cent and do well, so it was great for him. There was good news too for Kevin Yates, who pipped Rob Hardwick to the loose-head position for the Test. 'Yatesie' temporarily got us worried when he hobbled in on crutches one morning, but then he revealed all and explained that he was actually fine . . . it was all a ploy to help avoid some of the many potholes in the city!

That win against Argentina 'A' set us up perfectly for the Test match, which featured six new England caps starting the game. It also featured nine Bath players, seven of them in the England side. But while there were wide grins all round from the debutants, they were under no illusions that it would be an easy ride. Playing against Argentina would not be a soft debut cap. The Pumas are always a tough proposition, and having seen them cause plenty of upsets in the past with their own style of power play, we didn't want to be their next victims.

With so much talent in the England back row, competition was always likely to be tough. Saracens' Tony Diprose forced his way into the side at number eight, ahead of Chris Sheasby, and Martin Corry was called up to play as blind-side flanker – switching numbers with Ben Clarke, who moved to play at six. Nick Greenstock was always in pole position to win his place as the new centre, and, at 31 years old, 'gentleman Jim' Mallinder was rewarded with a debut cap at full-back.

So to the Ferrocarril Oeste stadium in Buenos Aires and a noisy crowd of 20,000 partisan locals, armed with firecrackers. Catty sent his opening kick-off way into touch, and we were on the back foot immediately. It meant that we were forced to play the game in our half for the first quarter, which made for a real contest. We were under a lot of pressure from the fast and mobile Pumas. Mervin Brewer from the *Observer* said that we'd 'rocked before we'd rolled', and during that first period we were definitely under the cosh. It needed a couple of telling defensive contributions from a rejuvenated Tony Diprose to calm things down. 'Dippy' had an outstanding game.

But when myself and Martin Corry made a break into the Argentinian half, Catty redeemed himself following his earlier mistake with a bit of his now-trademark chip-and-chase magic, and Nick Greenstock finished the move off to nudge us in front with his debut international try. Gonzalo Quesada kept the Pumas on our heels in a topsy-turvy first half when he nipped through from a lineout to score, and he added three points soon after with a 40-yard drop-goal. Argentinian hooker Freddie Méndez also made his mark before leaving the field with a dislocated shoulder, when his strong hand-off and subsequent pass to Reggiardo eventually led to a try by Lisandro Arbizu which momentarily put the Pumas in front at 10–13.

However, once we'd reorganised our defence and steadied the scrummage, we started to win better ball from the set pieces and the loose, and we 'rolled'. The boys began to gel together more effectively than anyone could have expected, and we started running at the Pumas. We went back in front during injury time in the first half thanks to a score by Tony Diprose. Mike Catt drifted across field and pulled the Pumas defence all over the place, creating a huge gap which Dippy exploited to perfection. That put us 17–13 ahead at the break and gave us a major psychological advantage. Our opponents were a spent force, and were never really in the game again. When the teams came out for the second half it was all England, and we scored three tries in a ten-minute spell which put the contest beyond doubt. I think the Argentinians were exhausted.

Ade Adebayo scored a superb running try under the posts, and from that moment on we really enjoyed the game. We played some wonderful rugby in the second half, with Ben driving in from close range and Catty stealing through for a score. Ade ran in a second to round the game off, and even though Solari pulled a try back, England were out of sight. With all of the debutants rising to the occasion, the scrum solid after an early wobble, and Haagie and Ollie holding their own in the lineout, it was a very satisfying performance from our supposedly 'scratch XV'. Richard Cockerill had become the seventh new England cap on the field when he replaced the injured Phil Greening after 25 minutes.

We were on a massive high after the six-try rout, so much so that the opening Test will remain in my mind for some time, and it was comfortably the highlight of the tour. Jack even went so far as to say that he felt the new-look England performance was one of the 'best ever', and it certainly left the critics in no doubt that we are already well on the way to having a powerful World Cup squad for '99. We came off the pitch really believing that we could win the second Test to go home with a record-breaking clean sweep in the inter-nationals.

The lads had a predictably good night after that. There's a Spanish way to celebrate, where you don't go out to eat before 1 a.m. and then you stay out till 5 a.m. – so we celebrated 'Español' after the Test! Admittedly, the guys who were playing again on the Tuesday took it a little easy, but we still had a great night. In fact, the Argentinian hospitality was always very good, and we were made to feel welcome everywhere we went throughout the trip. When we were in Mendoza we were shown around a local winery and our hosts couldn't do enough for us. We had a first-class meal and some excellent wine.

There wasn't a great deal of spare time on the trip and for the most part we were training, eating and playing. Our hotel was right in the heart of Buenos Aires city centre, so we didn't see much of the stunning countryside and there weren't too many distractions on offer either. We did go grand prix racing at the nearby amusement arcade, spend a few leisurely hours go-karting, and play ten holes of golf after the Buenos Aires game. But this first professional tour was quite rightly focused on the job of rugby.

I sat out the fifth and penultimate game of the tour against Cuyo on a rock-hard pitch in Mendoza, and although we didn't play particularly well we still managed to win 38–7. It was another very satisfying performance with the boys notching up our fourth victory out of five, particularly as Cuyo had beaten the English tourists in 1990 and because the names and faces in the England squad were now changing on a daily basis.

John Mallett and Phil Greening returned home sporting injuries, and Catty had left for South Africa on the Monday. Ollie promptly followed him to the Lions' den later on in the week, on the Thursday before the final deciding Test in the two-match series. The swings and roundabouts meant an England call for Steve Diamond, who jetted in as a late replacement just in time for the Cuyo game. He touched down at midday and was on the pitch in an international jersey for the kick-off at 2 p.m.! Will Green was another replacement who arrived late, although not quite as late as Steve. Will arrived on the Monday and he also played against Cuyo.

In the end Cuyo took some beating, despite the fact that they were fielding a young side and, like us, were well below full strength. Captain for the day, Chris Sheasby, eager to win back the England number eight shirt from Tony Diprose, was particularly impressive. With the team drawing inspiration from Chris it was another six-try haul, with Jim Mallinder scoring twice after he had replaced a hobbling Ade after half an hour. One of Jim's tries was an outstanding team effort, with five players involved in the move which started when Darren O'Leary intercepted a stray pass from Manuel Diaz.

The mounting injuries and the sudden loss of not one but two of our first-choice players to the Lions did nothing to enhance our prospects for the second Test. But while the England management was more than a little annoyed at the high-handedness of the Lions' approach, the attitude among the players in the camp nevertheless remained buoyant. With the journey home just a few days away, the players might have felt inclined to start winding down, albeit prematurely, with one crucial Test still to play. However, on this tour the attitude among the players was a real credit to them at all times, and it helped make the job of captaincy more straightforward. There was no complacency creeping into the England ranks, and having rattled the Pumas in our first encounter we knew that the Argentinians would come out fighting this time round.

They did. One week after we crushed the Pumas in the first Test, it was a completely different story in the second, and our hastily rearranged England team came in for a bit of a mauling. By the time we had kicked off again in the Ferrocarril Oeste stadium in Buenos Aires the list of new caps had risen to nine, with Mark Mapletoft and Danny Grewcock becoming the latest England internationals. That rose to ten when Alex King ran on to the field to play the last quarter.

Having been severely criticised after the initial defeat, Argentina changed their tactics, as we knew they would, and they came at us with a vengeance. The Pumas opted to kick the ball a lot more, both out of hand and at penalty situations, having not gone for goal from any one of 14 penalties in the first Test, and they also drove the ball more effectively in their forwards. Despite starting poorly we defended well for the first period, playing into a very strong wind. Quesada slotted a simple penalty in the opening moments after we had been caught well offside at a ruck, and that marked an important watershed: it was the only time on the entire six-match tour that we failed to strike first!

However, it could have been much worse. Myself and Haagie just got our hands under the ball to prevent Pumas flanker Fernandez-Lobbe touching down for the opening try of the game. After Quesada had missed two eminently kickable penalties and sliced a drop-goal attempt wide, he eventually found a bit of form and kicked a cracker from about 50 yards – the result of yet another offside infringement. That came on 25 minutes and made the score 0–6. Up until that point we'd spent little or no time in their half, so when Sleights rounded Soler and mounted an attack we thought we were back in the hunt. The move resulted in our first penalty but, unfortunately, 'Tofty' kicked the chance well wide.

Nevertheless, it was a schoolboy mix-up that really turned the game. We'd started to get things together and introduce some rhythm into our play when there was a cock-up between Jim Mallinder and Ade. The scissors move backfired big-time, with the ball dropping hopelessly short and going loose. Facundo Soler picked up the gift and scored from more than 40 yards. It's too late now – and it had nothing to do with the mistake or the Pumas try – but I don't really think that either Jim or Ade was fully fit. Ade had spent the latter part of the week on crutches to protect his injured ankle, and in the final event he only managed 67 minutes before being replaced by Andy Gomarsall.

Quesada finally slotted a conversion and although England went straight back down the other end of the pitch and pulled three points back, we went into half-time 3–13 adrift, rather than 3–6.

Playing into a fierce gusting wind I would have settled for 0–6 at the break. But it was not to be.

Even though we were playing with the wind at our backs in the second half, there were two further killer blows soon after the interval, with another successful Quesada penalty followed by a try, the result of a second England mistake. A loose kick out of defence gave the Argentinians an opportunity to mount a storming counter-attack, and Pumas prop Grau first threw a dummy and then scored what was, for him, a deserved try. Suddenly, having been just 3–6 down, we were staring down the abyss at 3–23, and there was no way back for our young team. It was one hill too many for our scratch team to climb. Further tries from Soler and Simone rubbed salt into the wounds, although we made a spirited comeback with late tries from Alex King and Danny Grewcock. Any hope of the England team writing itself into rugby history by returning home from an overseas tour with a 100 per cent Test record had evaporated. Instead our inexperience showed, and we suffered our heaviest defeat since losing 15–40 to the Aussies in 1991.

There were a few too many mistakes and that's all part of the learning curve for the new players. No excuses, and certainly no disgrace. They now know that you can't make those sort of errors at international level. But there were plenty of plus points too from the outstanding tour, so we weren't too downhearted after the defeat. At least it meant that we could enjoy the dinner afterwards! The Argentinians even introduced their singing prop to the evening's festivities. Hasan Jalil is a Puma who fancies himself as an opera singer – and there's no question, he really is talented. In response we gave them the musical doctor, Terry Crystal, another supreme vocalist. They both got up to sing at the end of the meal, closely followed by Mike Slemen, who gave us a great rendition of 'You'll Never Walk Alone'. Then the ref, Ian Rogers, gave us a tune, with both teams joining in as and when they could. It was a superb occasion. We sang for almost an hour before leaving, and there was a great atmosphere. Then German Llanes pointed us in the direction of the best nightclub in town and we went on to 'blood' the new England caps. The Pumas left for a six-match tour of New Zealand the following day, so they were soon home to bed. However, we didn't have to leave until late on the Sunday, and so we had plenty of time to recover before the long flight!

More than a handful of new England players took their chances during the tour, and some older hands staked and restaked their claims. Tony Diprose played very well on the trip. He's a good distributor of the ball. Even before we left for Argentina I felt that he might be one of the players to really come through. Dippy has been there or thereabouts for a while, and he proved his worth.

Kyran Bracken started the tour as he meant to go on and played very sharply in the opening game against Cordoba. He was back to his best and proved himself as a top-quality scrum-half both in attack and in defence. In the centre it was good to see Wasps' Nick Greenstock come through. Nick is young but I reckon he has a big future playing for England, and I hope it all goes well for him.

Kevin Yates seized his chance with both hands, and David Rees played well on the wing. Richard Cockerill did an outstanding job, and Ben Clarke played himself back into serious contention for a regular place in the side. The tour worked wonders for Ben. He was on good form on and off the field, and is back to his bruising best. Haagie, too, was terrific, and he managed to win nearly all of his own ball in the lineouts, as well as some of theirs. He also made his mark as a good ball-handler and an excellent runner in broken-field play. He's pushing hard.

On the flip side there were a few players who must have come home somewhat disappointed. Alex King and Andy Gomarsall were not on top form, although Alex got better as the tour went on after a poor first game against Cordoba – a good sign. Mark Mapletoft played well at full-back, but was out of sorts playing at fly-half in the second Test match. It's pretty hard when you have to step up in class. The game is played at a different pace and you always need time to adjust.

As for me personally, I was very happy with my contribution. I scored a couple of tries and played consistently, as well as performing well as captain. I believe that I also succeeded in earning the respect of the England players who made the trip, an important achievement for any captain. It is a demanding role, particularly on an overseas tour. Players rely on the skipper for help, advice and information. They want to know when and where things are going to happen, from dinner right through to team selection and match tactics. You're the captain for the whole trip, and you know it! But I came back having enjoyed the tour, so it must have gone well.

In this respect we were helped by the tour back-up, which was excellent. Administratively things have really progressed, so much so that the quality of the back-up was one of the best features of the whole tour. Dave Redding was superb as our fitness adviser. He spent most of his time keeping the squad members who were not involved in the next match focused on maintaining their fitness levels. Our three-man medical team was with us all the way, and so too was kicking coach Mark Tainton. I benefited from his input, as did many of the other players. However, perhaps the most significant step in the right direction came from an unexpected quarter. The England tourists included a referee in the party, Chris White, whose input proved to be outstanding. After games Chris was able to break down the important plays for us, and also explain things from a referee's point of view. In addition he was able to talk to the match referees in advance, and get some clarification about how they wanted to see the games played. It was the first time we have taken a referee away with us on an overseas tour and his involvement proved invaluable.

This has been an interesting discussion point since we returned. In the future I think all senior clubs should appoint an affiliated referee who can help with training, coaching and talking to the players about the rules. It can only help improve the bond between referees and players. Every area already has its own referee, but, for instance, Tony Spreadbury never referees his home team, Bath, because he lives there. However, his input is already proving valuable to the team. The same would surely be true with Chris White at Gloucester, Ed Morrison at Bristol and so on. We should talk to referees much more than we do at present, and we should try to get the rapport going.

As far as the RFU were concerned, John Richardson and his wife were out in Argentina and they mixed particularly well with the squad. Graham Smith was also out there and he too fitted in – a real players' man.

At the end of the tour Jack said that he had been 'pleased and privileged' to be the manager on the trip. It spoke volumes about the commitment and professionalism of the guys involved, and about how well we had worked together. The passion and spirit were also great, and said a lot about our future international prospects.

These days we are all so much better technically, and that helped when it came to introducing the new international caps. Since the domestic game turned professional our progress has accelerated, and we've managed to develop strength in depth. The evidence is there for all to see. Young players like Matt Allen and Jos Baxendell really do have a bright international future, and it bodes well for the English game.

In retrospect, I would have settled for a shared 1–1 series, given that many of our key players were injured or elsewhere. Despite their subsequent heavy defeat at the hands of the awesome All Blacks, Argentina are a growing force in the world of rugby, and certainly no walkover. 'It was another step on the road to challenging the world's best,' said Hugh Godwin in *The Sunday Times*. We came home with our heads held high, proud of the contribution of our talented young team.

That's why it's such a shame that question marks remain over the managerial future of England boss Jack Rowell, whose current international contract expires in August 1997. I find it very odd, and not a little disappointing, to hear the RFU sending out signals which indicate that Jack may not be invited to stay on. I can't see how they can sack him on the basis of his record, which is excellent. We capped 17 new players in the 1996–97 season, ten of them in Argentina, and England won six out of nine internationals under his management, losing only three – to New Zealand Barbarians, France and the Pumas, the last a 'tidal wave of a challenge' with an inexperienced team. Surely that's not bad by anyone's standards? But if there are still doubts then they should not be made public. Wisely, Jack has kept his own counsel. Unfortunately others have not.

When we arrived home, we were looking forward to playing the Aussies in a one-off Test in July. We knew it wouldn't be easy to get the balance right in the squad between the England tourists who played in Argentina and the English Lions, who were exhausted after their gruelling trip. We didn't even get to see our Lions before we got to Australia.

Luckily(!) the Bath contingent had the 'gentle encouragement' of fitness coach Jim Blair, who was already cracking the whip. There was no chance that any of us would go to seed in the month-long gap between the two summer tours. As soon as Jim arrived we knew there would be no messing. He flew in on the Sunday, 24 hours before the England team got back to the UK from Argentina. We'd already been told in advance that Jim would like to assess our fitness on the Wednesday, giving us one day clear to relax and recover from the long flight. But when myself and Sleights phoned Robbo in the car on the way back from Heathrow, the short call left us in no doubt that Jim is the right man to turn us into the fittest club side around in good time for the new domestic season. Robbo told us that Jim would be assessing our fitness first thing on the Tuesday morning and, despite our protests, we were there at 10 a.m. And it was hard.

We have now been given individual programmes. Although I may be resting from physical contact, as I'm not playing, in many ways I'm working harder than ever on my fitness, training five or six times a week rather than three times a week during the season.

I know I speak for all of us when I say that the boys at Bath RFC want to be winners again in 1997–98, and we know that to do this we have to be in peak physical condition. Jim Blair will be making certain of that. When he gathered us together for the first time, the conversation opened with, 'Fellas, we don't meet at 10 a.m., we start at 10 a.m., so make sure you're all ready.' We also know that we need to be even fitter than we are at present. So when Jim added, straight-faced, 'If you fuck me about, mate, I'll cut your throat,' we gulped hard and got our heads down. I'm looking forward to seeing him 'beast' some of the guys who aren't as fit as they should be. They'll have to respond because he won't take any prisoners . . .

CHAPTER ELEVEN

De Glanville on de Glanville

You couldn't get two more different people than myself and Jerry Guscott, and perhaps that's why our centre partnership for Bath has worked so well for so long. I think it's true that your personality reflects the way you play the game, and our very different characters and sporting skills complement each other well, combining to create a fluid and effective rugby partnership which has blossomed at club level.

I have a lot of time and respect for Jerry. He's a close mate, and a wonderful player. But as a person he's a selfish bastard, and occasionally that comes through in his rugby. It's not always a drawback on the field; indeed, very often it's an asset. When Jerry gets the ball in an attacking situation and he sees an opening, or when he is on a mission to score, there are very few teams which can stop him.

That capacity to be selfish is evident in all aspects of his life, not just on the rugby field – and he knows it! Jerry would probably be the first to come clean. However, in recent seasons Jerry has become noticeably less selfish as a rugby player, and he has also been increasingly willing to put himself on the line for the sake of his teammates. It has added an extra dimension to his game.

My personality and skills complement those of my playing partner. He feeds very well off the de Glanville service. My greatest strength as a player is in support play, backing people up and being in the right position at the right time. I am good at being the link man in a break, keeping my head and taking the right option. If I make the break, I'm good at making sure that the move is finished off – and not necessarily by me. I'm the man giving Jerry Guscott the bullets to fire.

173

Perhaps I should be a little more selfish and finish off some of the moves myself. I've often been encouraged to take more opponents on one-to-one, and to 'have a go' on my own account. But that's not the way I've been taught to play rugby union. I generally prefer to beat the oncoming player with a pass, rather than running past or through him. Sometimes it means that my valuable support work can go unnoticed because other players are grabbing the limelight, although I just call it good teamwork.

However, I reckon I'm more than just a link man between the number ten and the wings. I have sound rugby instincts, and my decision-making under pressure is generally very good. It's those decision-making and leadership skills, honed by two seasons at the helm with Bath, which have ultimately given me the chance to captain my country.

I also enjoy putting pressure on the opposition's defence, and I am, and always have been, a strong, brave tackler. I don't mind getting into the thick of the action. Just take one look at my rugby player's nose, which tells the story of many a close-fought battle! There have been seven breaks thanks to stray boots and knees. That's why some close friends have come to nickname me 'Hammer' rather than 'Hollywood'! Despite the cool, calm and collected presence of the predator Jerry Guscott always on my shoulder, I still manage to score more than my fair share of tries at club and now at England level, proving that I too am no mean finisher when it's required.

Some of my rugby-playing qualities suggest that I might have made a more natural open-side flanker, rather than a centre. I suppose I do have some of the skills required by an open-side flanker, and my father played in that position for some years. Perhaps it's in the genes? I do like to be involved for the whole of a game, and occasionally at centre you can spend long periods without being in the thick of the action. However, I have no regrets.

Since becoming a captain, I have added some new dimensions to my own game. I've developed a much greater understanding of what everybody else is doing on the pitch, and of what we should be trying to achieve from certain positions. The technical and man-

management skills I have learned and fine-tuned as the Bath skipper were essential for my further success with England, and throughout the 1996–97 season I learned new tricks and techniques which I can put to good use in the future. But I won't be captaining Bath in 1997–98. There's no rocket science to this decision. It's just that I've done it for two years, and every Bath captain going back to Roger Spurrell has captained the side for no more than a two-year stint. I think the time is right for someone new to do the job, and Andy Nicol is the man taking on that mantle.

It has nothing to do with the pressure of holding both the Bath and the England captaincy. Yes, it is harder to do them both well because there is a lot to do, and I did consider giving up the Bath captaincy late one dark winter night in the middle of the Five Nations Championship. I felt then that perhaps it would be better for Bath to have someone who was dedicated to the club at all times. But as it would be somewhat premature for me to assume that I am going to be the England captain for this coming season, that conflict of interest has nothing to do with my decision to give up my captain's armband at Bath. It's simply the right time for a change.

However, if I am reappointed as England skipper, I am probably going to have to do more than ever in what is another very busy international season. We have four major internationals before Christmas – the big ones against Australia, New Zealand twice and South Africa – and I would need to be focused on those massive encounters. Equally, there are more club games than ever before in the hectic domestic and European schedule, and the Bath captaincy needs and deserves someone who is dedicated 100 per cent. I could not give that time if I am still wearing the England captain's armband, because those two demanding roles are now growing too big for one man.

To date I have enjoyed both success and silverware in my chosen sporting career, but I have only achieved this success by putting in a huge effort and by remaining patient. It hasn't always come easily, although people often assume that I was 'born with a silver spoon in my mouth' by virtue of my privileged education and lack of a local

West Country accent. Perhaps I do look more like a suited business-man than a rough and ready rugby player, and this is reflected by a few of the nicknames I've picked up over the years – 'Hollywood' and 'Blouse', in particular. But I've brought that businesslike approach to my game, and have worked hard at what I do. I'm very conscientious. If I make a commitment I try my best to keep it, and I don't mess people around. I think I have a very professional attitude to rugby, although having said that I still try to be quite relaxed about the role the sport plays in my life. You have to keep a sense of perspective about things, and be prepared to laugh at yourself. For instance, the recent Phil de Glanville Nike advertise-ment caused a certain amount of amusement among my mates in London. Rather than using the original copy line, 'Play Hard and Fast', some of my commuter friends in London – who saw it again and again over a long period of time on the underground – were ringing up to speak to their pal, 'Play Soft and Slow'.

I can still relax and have a laugh, but with the focus continually on the England captain, as a player, a captain and a person, it does become more difficult to switch off from the demanding world of professional top-flight rugby. In the past I never used to spend my Sundays thinking about how well (or not!) I'd played on a Saturday, but last season I found myself analysing the plays of the day before – the successes and the mistakes. You can't help thinking, 'If only I'd done that.' It feels like the media spotlight is shining brightly on my every move, and, while it is, there will probably be someone hoping that I'll make a mistake.

That's no exaggeration. I never thought about this aspect before and, in the past, none of this nonsense would have even crossed my mind. But I now need to be careful in public, and it's difficult to be on guard all of the time. You need to develop a 'sixth sense', and I'm still developing mine! Hence my gaff about Lions boss Fran Cotton at the Cambridge Union earlier this year. I thought I was chatting to a few friendly, sport-loving students about life as a rugby player, when one member of the small audience asked me a question about Fran and the Lions tour to South Africa. I thought nothing of it when I gave my candid reply . . . until it appeared in the headlines of the sports pages of the nationals the next day.

At one of the England 'A' games last season, I sat in the stand shouting some friendly abuse at my clubmates on the pitch. There's nothing wrong with that. Indeed, it's something I've always done and probably always will do. Yet one spectator turned round and asked me to stop, because I was the England captain. It makes you wonder.

Some people like to carry all the burden on their own shoulders and feel that they can't offload, by telling anybody. I'm lucky, because I've got loved ones to whom I can turn. Yes, I feel I can cope, and will be able to cope, with the job on my own. But, if it is the case, I would never be afraid to say that it is getting too much for me, and that I need help. Asking for that help is a very personal thing, and I always lean on my wife and parents for the emotional support that I need.

Rugby has always been an integral part of my life, and certainly my life with Yolanda, who has lived with the game ever since I met her. The sport, and my enormous commitment to it, doesn't create any tension whatsoever between us, and that's just one of many ways in which I'm very lucky indeed. Like all of us, Yolanda loves the social side of the game, and the wives and girlfriends of the Bath players share the same sort of camaraderie as the players themselves. It really is a family, and all of us at the club are there for each other.

It's quite interesting to look at rugby players' wives and girlfriends, as they tend to be pretty similar in many key respects. They have no problem in looking after themselves, because they are used to being on their own, and they can also give and take stick with the best. Most of them are positive, strong women, and know exactly what they want out of life. And, perhaps most importantly, they all know how to party! I met more than my match with Yolanda.

I am also helped by the almost 'happy-go-lucky' approach my family and close friends have taken to my rugby days with Bath, and to the England captaincy in particular. When the debate about the appointment began in the newspapers, my mother refused to comment. Her attitude was, 'What will happen, will happen'. That really helps. There has never been any pressure on me to achieve, but all of my close family are nevertheless behind me every step of the way. My wife, parents and sister are immensely proud, and that came through at the Italy game, my first as captain. They were beaming.

Although I don't feel under any undue pressure at the moment, I am still aware that I'm approaching a crucial period in my life, where I can see my priorities changing, although it may be two or three years away yet. My priorities are inevitably going to shift from rugby to family when Yolanda and I have children. Added to that, I have always taken a relatively short-term view of the England captaincy. This is only sensible for a man in his late-20s; after all, professional sportsmen are having to peak younger and retire earlier than ever before, even when injuries don't intervene.

That's why I am going to enjoy my rugby as much as I can, for as long as I can. And while I'm doing so, I'll be saving up for the day when I'm no longer running out on to the pitch. Nowadays I've got a chance to do that as we're earning good money – although perhaps not as much as some of the pundits make out! Four years ago I can remember 'earning' £5,000, my share of the monies pooled from the England players' promotional and marketing activity. It was all we 'earned' for the whole season. In the year before we went professional, that figure crept up to £10,000 after tax – a lot of money – and, genuinely, the only income we received from rugby apart from normal expenses. We were very grateful for it. When I first went to Bath in 1990 I didn't even get travel expenses, as I lived in the city. There was never any talk of payments. How the game has changed.

My current job at Druid came directly through Bath rugby. The company were looking out for a high-profile rugby player with a proven marketing background, and they approached Bath RFC to see whether the club had anyone suitable on their books. Bath recommended me for an interview, and I got the job. It has worked out superbly, and I could not have asked for any more from Druid. Their commercial director, John Pocock, has been superb, and he is always helpful. They have been so good that it sometimes makes me feel guilty. It may sound cheesy, but it's true.

But you have to be fair and realistic these days, even when there is so much more money rushing around the veins of the rugby world. As Bath RFC made the initial introduction, my Druid salary is taken into account in my club rugby contract. In terms of hard cash, that means I'm probably on the lower end of the Bath pay scale. However, my income from England appearances and other earnings is more than enough compensation.

As far as I am concerned, the best thing of all is that I am still working, albeit one day a week, and that I have not been forced into full-time rugby thanks to the flexibility and approach of Druid. I don't want to stop work and, unlike some of my Bath teammates who have come under increasing pressure to make that difficult choice, I do not intend to give up my job without a fight. At the moment, and with Druid's help, I'm managing to juggle my responsibilities, but I won't have to do that for ever.

The way Yolanda and myself have approached my 'new' role in the England team (and my rugby in general) is that it could well be 'here today, gone tomorrow', and that we need to enjoy the good times and make the most of them while they last. We've seen players, and captains, come and go in all international team sports. There is no room for sentiment or loyalty, and rightly so. We regard the money as terrific, but we have been very careful not to regard it as a long-term income stream. You've got to look on the money as a bonus, otherwise it will all end in tears.

The newspapers quoted figures of £70–£80,000 per man for last year's England campaign, but it wasn't that much, and the maximum payments were only made to players who played in all the games and had a full set of 'win bonuses' to collect. I missed the game against Argentina, and there were two defeats along the way, so the actual figure last season was considerably less. As always, the finances need to be set in a wider context, because I could be injured or dropped tomorrow.

Today, rugby players have been cast as professional sportsmen. They are gradually learning to plan their day-to-day approach towards the new game, and to live up to its increased demands. But they will also need to plan, personally and financially, for the 'retirement' years afterwards, because, one way or another, a rugby career won't last for ever. You now need a sensible, 'professional' game plan, and although I'm the England captain, I'm no different from anyone else in this respect.

One day my England and Bath playing days will be over. There are plenty of talented young players pressing for places, and it's going to be tough all the way if I want to keep my place in either squad. The stakes are now higher than ever, and the competition for all positions is intense. That of course, is good for the future health of the game. But all being well, I still reckon that I've got two more seasons left in the top flight, and that would fit in with my current three-year Bath contract, of which there are now two years left to run. So, injuries and form permitting, I can go on playing at the Rec until the 1998–99 season. I'll be 31. And what then?

Yolanda and I have always talked about going to live overseas for two or three years, and, for me, that means playing my twilight rugby years abroad. At some point I think we would like to go and live in Italy, and to play rugby there. The timing of that would have to be right; I would still need to be able to make a positive contribution on the field.

Why Italy? Yolanda is half Spanish, and she speaks Italian. It's a move that would be good for us, and also for our children – when we get round to having them! From the kids' point of view a bilingual upbringing could make a big difference in their lives. Yolanda spoke Spanish until she was five years old and it has certainly helped her over the years. Italy is therefore a distinct possibility, but I've got no real desire to go any further, even if I was asked – and I haven't been. Any of the southern hemisphere rugby-playing countries are just too far away for the de Glanvilles.

I don't think that I'll be the only rugby player moving overseas either. Although we've seen plenty of foreign rugby stars moving to the UK of late, there hasn't been any trade the other way. But, before too much longer, I expect to see talented homegrown players making the move abroad, particularly if they are being squeezed out of regular first-team rugby here. To date we haven't seen players moving to France or Italy, but it will happen. If good young players can't get a first-team game for Bath, Leicester or Wasps, or there's a top foreign star playing in their position, they'll move and go to play elsewhere – perhaps in South Africa or New Zealand. It will herald a new two-way process which will no doubt see some top players playing a winter in the southern hemisphere, followed by a winter in the northern hemisphere, and year-round rugby union will have an interesting effect on the game. It happened in rugby league, and there's no reason to think that it won't happen in the union code.

If the de Glanvilles stay at home and don't go abroad, I'm sure that plenty of other business and professional opportunities will arise. My work with Druid is going well, and there is always the possibility of a move into a business role in rugby, although I have to admit to being somewhat cautious about working too closely with my father at Rhino, at least for the moment. Working with relatives can be a minefield! I certainly couldn't start writing about rugby on a regular basis either, a move made by some other well-known ex-rugby players. I wouldn't mind writing a general over-view of a game, or commentating once in a while, but I don't think I would like to take a critical look at a player's performance. I don't want to have to find something controversial to say about an ex-colleague or a friend just to make a name for myself or to earn a few bob.

My rugby career could well end in the Italian sunshine. But what will happen in the world of rugby, and what would I like to see? In the long term, the most important thing for the game of rugby union is that it must try to become self-financing. Rugby must find its 'own level' where it can pay the wages, plan for the future and make ground improvements without outside funding. The top clubs can't go on taking more and more money from a handful of generous entrepreneurs in the belief that they will continue to finance and support rugby simply because they love the game. Life is not like that.

Wasps' benefactor Chris Wright, the multi-millionaire boss of the Chrysalis records, video and TV empire, purchased the club as a business opportunity. Initially he was not a rugby fan, although he's come to love the sport during his first season in charge, a Courage

League Championship-winning season. But Wasps won't win the Premiership every year and, in the future, I'm sure that everything won't seem so rosy as far as Mr Wright is concerned. Although I have no doubt that he is now a committed rugby fan, money makes the world go round. Because that has always been the case in the past and always will be in the future, Chris Wright and the other club owners will soon want to start seeing some serious financial return, so the books will have to balance.

Gate monies will therefore have to be increased over time. But you can't increase ticket prices without a simultaneous and dramatic improvement in ground facilities, and at most rugby grounds these facilities are still terrible. Rugby is a generation behind in comparison with soccer. This is the area where real money now needs to be invested in our game, not in bringing more and more highly paid, glitzy international players to these shores. The senior clubs are going to find the harsh realities of business life very hard indeed, and making the books balance will be an issue which will soon overtake the salary battle. At some clubs it's already the primary issue, and one thing's for sure: there are some top clubs which will go bust as a result.

I think that the summer of 1997 has already been an important period of consolidation as far as professionalism is concerned, certainly for Bath and no doubt for all the other leading clubs. After one hell of a first year of professionalism, I am hopeful that the administration and the administrators will all be working in the same direction. The formation of the English Rugby Partnership (ERP), jointly owned by the RFU (50 per cent), English First Division Rugby (33.3 per cent) and English Second Division Rugby (16.6 per cent), has been a step forward, and the players do have representation on that company, with Wasps' Damian Hopley attending board meetings.

Over the last six months I think the RFU have been improving their attitude, but, on reflection, I am not sure that all of the considerable pressure put on them, first by the WRC and then by EPRUC, has necessarily moved the ball in 'our' favour. The continual wrangling over the last two seasons has actually made the

RFU even more introverted; there's almost a siege mentality at HQ. But I have come to believe that unless the RFU are put under pressure they won't concede anything. However, not everybody at the RFU should be held to blame, and things are improving with time.

The first offspring of the still-fledgling ERP is the £12 million, three-year sponsorship package of League Divisions One and Two signed by financial services company Allied Dunbar. The new competition is the Allied Dunbar Premiership, One and Two, but there are still 24 teams competing in the two leagues. That means no change in the heavy schedule of games planned, at least for the 1997–98 season. But something has to give, or else our leading players will be burned out before their time and we'll never match the teams from the southern hemisphere, who play far fewer games of a far higher standard. Last season I remember feeling desperately tired from playing so many games, and I also felt in need of a break – mental as well as physical. This season it's going to be worse.

I welcome an extension of the European club competition but it must be at the expense of domestic league games. We either need to halve the league games to 11 and play home *or* away, or cut the number of teams in the Premiership right down to eight so that we would play 14 games, home and away. That would be my preference because I think it would also help make it a proper, more exclusive Premiership competition. The best players would play for those eight clubs, and we would automatically be playing big games every week. It would be real Super 12s stuff in terms of standards, and I reckon that it would be very competitive. There would probably be teams losing up to four or five games a season but still in with a chance of winning the Premiership. Every game would be the equivalent of a cup final.

I think most people are in agreement that there are too many fixtures. Now we need to see action to cut down the number of fixtures and introduce a sensible policy which will reduce all playing commitments. In my view, it's the Premiership that has got to give, because we still need a domestic cup competition to allow the smaller clubs their moment of glory, and because those European

Cup games will all be crucial in helping to raise the standards of our club rugby. It's a bold decision we have to take, bearing in mind the commercial implications, but it's a decision that needs to be taken for the benefit of the game.

Once the number of games has been addressed, the next three most important jobs on the agenda should be the introduction of a regulated transfer market, the formation of an independent disciplinary body, and a detailed look at the way our referees are rated and selected. At Bath all of the current playing staff have a two- or three-year contract. Nobody will be moving, at least not in the short term. But unless a well-thought-out administrative structure is put into place soon which covers transfer fees and the transfer market, the game could again sink into chaos. Once transfer payments are a factor as well as salaries, finances could escalate beyond control, and it could end up in a situation where the top stars take the lion's share of the money, without much cash being left for the players and the clubs further down the pecking order. When the current club contracts are up, all hell will break loose unless there is a proper transfer system in place, with sensible deadlines.

New Zealand have only recently introduced a transfer system, and they have been professional for a few years. The Kiwis have a system where the club which releases the player gets a proportion of the transfer money, linked to how far the player is moving up the playing ladder. That's one way to do it. However, the key thing is for the RFU to think about this now before it's too late, and to put something into action which is relevant to the entire game.

Secondly, I would certainly like to see an independent arbitrator who would deal with disciplinary matters. I suffered a really horrific gash to the eye when playing for the South-west against the All Blacks in 1993. It needed 15 stitches, and could have cost me a place in the famous Test team which beat the New Zealanders 15–9 at Twickenham. That was a memorable victory which still ranks as one of the highlights of my career, not least because it was my first starting game for England and because the All Blacks had thrashed Scotland the week before. But I was lucky to make the team. The injury was really nasty. I had made a half-tackle, and three or four other players arrived on the scene, we slewed around, and the maul fell. I was lying on someone else, perhaps halfway up, and I knew that I was on the wrong side and in a dangerous position. But I was given a good rucking. I know who it was, and it was obvious to anyone watching the TV footage. But no action was ever taken against the perpetrator, despite an RFU letter to the New Zealand Rugby Union. 'It was an accident,' the New Zealanders said, 'and all part of the game.' There needs to be a neutral body to oversee these matters. In a professional game, we should be treating breaches of discipline seriously. After all, players' careers are at stake.

The third item on my 'wish list' for the (near) future concerns referees. I feel there should be match-by-match player/coach feedback about referees; a system which encourages consistency. The referee can determine the outcome of a game, so it's vital that we have the best men possible in charge of games, particularly now the stakes are so high. It's not so much a tightening-up of standards that is required − referees are only human − but a system whereby referees receive regular feedback about their performances from players as well as the assessors, so that they can improve.

My specific concern is that there is little or no consistency. For example, one referee we encountered in the 1996–97 season assured us before the game that he was going to be 'really hard' on offside offences and players diving over the ball, and yet he let both offences go time and again during the game. Refs need people to tell them what is good and bad from the playing point of view. At the moment they get nothing constructive back from the players, and that's not their fault. That whole feedback process needs to be improved, upgraded and generally made more professional, so that refs receive regular reports rather than relying on what they learn from occasional one-off conferences.

Someone recently said to me that we could eventually end up with three different games of rugby: semi-professional rugby league, amateur rugby union and a professional hybrid of the two, with the potent cocktail of money and television having forced the two codes together at the highest level. I can't see either the players or the supporters forcing the codes to merge. The games and their cultures are still so different, and so too is the way you are brought up to play rugby union and rugby league. Even the playing and physical skills involved are very different, something I learned from Bath's one and only bruising rugby league encounter against the mighty Wigan. Those two games against Wigan, one played under rugby league rules and the other under rugby union rules, broke down many of the age-old barriers between the codes, and where there was once hostility – much of it on the side of the purist rugby union supporters – there is now respect on both sides. We prepared well and worked hard in both of the games as a matter of pride, and then we went our separate ways, with a friendly parting handshake (and the phone numbers of a few Wigan stars!).

But one day it might be more than that. If the mega-rich global television moguls have a grand plan to merge the two codes you should not rule out the possibility of a hybrid, which would almost certainly be tested in the trend-setting southern hemisphere. If it worked there, and the money were made available, how could we minnows resist the power and influence of the money men and stand in the way of 'popular' change?

Yes, there are still tremendous differences between the players, the rules, the spectators, the culture and the traditions, and it would be difficult – and tragic – to lose some of our rugby union heritage. The game has given me so much and I love it, no question. But the world of sport is changing, and if the new hybrid game was good to watch, and the public voted it popular with its feet and TV viewing time, who knows what the future could hold . . . a whole new ball game?

PHILIP DE GLANVILLE

Senior Honours

Season	Fixture	Result	Score	Notes
1989–90	Italy B v. England B	Won	0–44	
1990–91	England B v. Namibia	Won	31–16	
	England B v. Spain	Won	50–6	
1991–92	Spain v. England B	Won	6–34	
	England B v. Ireland B	Won	47–15	
	France B v. England B	Won	18–22	
	Italy B v. England B	Won	10–16	
	New Zealand XV v. England B	Lost	24–18	
	New Zealand XV v. England B	Lost	26–18	1 try
1992–93	Leicester v. England XV	Won	11–18	Replacement
	England B v. South Africans	Lost	16–20	
	England v. South Africa	Won	33–16	Replacement
	Wales v. England	Lost	10–9	Replacement
1993–94	England v. New Zealand	Won	15–9	
	Scotland v. England	Won	14–15	
	England v. Ireland	Lost	12–13	
	France v. England	Won	14–18	
	England v. Wales	Won	15–8	

1994	*England tour to South Africa*			
	South Africa v. England	Won	15–32	
	South Africa v. England	Lost	27–9	

Season	Fixture	Result	Score	Notes
1994–95	England v. Canada	Won	60–19	Replacement
1995	*World Cup*			
	England v. Argentina	Won	24–18	Replacement
	England v. Italy	Won	27–20	
	England v. Western Samoa	Won	44–22	
1995–96	England v. South Africa	Lost	14–24	Replacement, 1 try
	England v. Wales	Won	21–15	Replacement
	England v. Ireland	Won	28–15	Replacement
1996–97	England v. Italy	Won	54–21	
	England v. Scotland	Won	41–13	1 try
	Ireland v. England	Won	6–46	
	England v. France	Lost	20–23	
	Wales v. England	Won	13–34	1 try
1997	*England tour to Argentina*			
	Argentina v. England	Won	46–20	
	Argentina v. England	Lost	13–33	
	Australia v. England	Lost	25–6	

PHILIP DE GLANVILLE

Bath Ist XV – Appearance Record

Season	Total	Courage League	Pilkington Cup	Heineken European Cup	Anglo-Welsh Cup	Friendly
1988–89	1					1
1989–90	1					1
1990–91	11	5	1			5
1991–92	21	10	5			6
1992–93	17	12	1			4
1993–94	21	15	5			1
1994–95	22	16	5			1
1995–96	24	17	5			2
1996–97	22	17	1	2	1	1
Totals	140	92	23	2	1	22

PHILIP DE GLANVILLE

Bath Ist XV Scoring Record – All Games

Season	Tries	Points
1988–89		
1989–90		
1990–91	8	32
1991–92	7	28
1992–93	4	20
1993–94	7	35
1994–95	5	25
1995–96	8	40
1996–97	4	20
Totals	43	200

BATH RUGBY FOOTBALL CLUB

1996–97 Season Record

Date	Opponent	Venue	Result	Score
COURAGE LEAGUE ONE				
31 Aug	Orrell v. Bath	A	Won	13–56
07 Sep	Leicester v. Bath	A	Lost	28–25
14 Sep	Bath v. Wasps	H	Lost	36–40
21 Sep	Gloucester v. Bath	A	Won	29–45
28 Sep	Bath v. West Hartlepool	H	Won	46–10
05 Oct	London Irish v. Bath	A	Won	31–56
29 Oct	Bath v. Bristol	H	Won	76–7
09 Nov	Northampton v. Bath	A	Lost	9–6
07 Dec	Bath v. Harlequins	H	Won	35–20
04 Jan	Bath v. Saracens	H	Won	35–33
11 Jan	Harlequins v. Bath	A	Lost	22–6
19 Jan	Bath v. Northampton	H	Won	52–14
22 Feb	Bristol v. Bath	A	Won	13–18
08 Mar	Bath v. London Irish	H	Won	46–3
27 Mar	West Hartlepool v. Bath	A	Won	16–24
02 Apr	Sale v. Bath	A	Lost	11–5
06 Apr	Wasps v. Bath	A	Drawn	25–25
12 Apr	Bath v. Leicester	H	Won	47–9
19 Apr	Bath v. Orrell	H	Won	40–14
26 Apr	Bath v. Sale	H	Won	84–7
30 Apr	Bath v. Gloucester	H	Won	71–21
03 May	Saracens v. Bath	A	Lost	36–29

League position: Second, 31 points

Date	Opponent	Venue	Result	Score
PILKINGTON CUP				
21 Dec	Bath v. London Irish	H	Won	33–0
08 Feb	Bath v. Leicester	H	Lost	28–39
HEINEKEN EUROPEAN CUP				
Pool A				
12 Oct	Bath v. Edinburgh	H	Won	55–26
19 Oct	Pontypridd v. Bath	A	Lost	19–6
26 Oct	Bath v. Dax	H	Won	25–16
02 Nov	Benetton Treviso v. Bath	A	Won	27–50
Quarter-final				
16 Nov	Cardiff v. Bath	A	Lost	22–19
ANGLO–WELSH TOURNAMENT				
11 Sep	Bath v. Swansea	H	Won	87–15
01 Oct	Llanelli v. Bath	A	Drawn	10–10
TOURING SIDES				
02 Dec	Bath v. Western Samoa	H	Won	36–17
04 Feb	Bath v. Otago	H	Lost	18–31
FRIENDLIES				
25 May	Bath v. Wigan	Twickenham	Won	44–19
22 Nov	Coventry v. Bath	A	Won	17–45
26 Nov	Bath v. Combined Services	H	Won	40–20
14 Dec	Bath v. Wakefield	H	Won	71–20
14 Feb	Bridgend v. Bath	A	Lost	26–3
25 Mar	Bath v. Army	H	Won	26–16
RUGBY LEAGUE				
08 May	Wigan v. Bath	Manchester City FC	Lost	82–6